The future of European Gas Markets

Claeys & Casteels Publishers

About the Fondazione Eni Enrico Mattei (FEEM)

Fondazione Eni Enrico Mattei (FEEM) is a research institution and a think tank, whose mission is to foster, through studies, research, scientific dissemination, information and training, a better understanding of sustainable development, and to improve the quality of decision-making in public and private spheres.

FEEM pursues its mission by promoting excellence, scientific rigor, the value of ideas and innovation in all its activities in collaboration with numerous partners that form an increasingly wide international network.

About FEEM's Energy Scenarios and Policy (ESP) research programme

The ESP research programme aims to carry out interdisciplinary, scientifically sound, prospective and policy-oriented applied research, targeted at political and business decision makers.

This aim is achieved through an integrated quantitative and qualitative analysis of energy scenarios and policies. This innovative and interdisciplinary approach puts together the major factors driving the change in global energy dynamics (i.e. technology, economy, geopolitics and sociological aspects). The ESP programme applies this methodology to a wide range of issues (energy demand and supply, infrastructures, financing, market analyses, socio-economic impacts of energy policies) that are explored from economic, geopolitical and institutional perspectives.

FONDAZIONE ENI ENRICO MATTEI

The Future of European Gas Markets

Balancing act between decarbonisation and security of supply

Manfred Hafner and Simone Tagliapietra

Claeys & Casteels Publishers

ISBN 978-90-77644-36-2

The paper and board used in the production of this book
is sourced exclusively from replanted forests.

Published in 2016 by

Claeys & Casteels Law Publishers
Deventer (Netherlands) - Leuven (Belgium)

P.O. Box 2013
7420 AA Deventer
Netherlands
www.claeys-casteels.com

Contents

Introduction

Gas represents a pivotal element of the European energy architecture. Covering about a quarter of the European total primary energy supply, it indeed represents the second-largest fuel in the European energy mix after oil.

The European gas markets are nowadays rapidly changing due to political, commercial and geopolitical evolutions. The evolution of the EU Energy Union, the EU-Russia gas relations in the aftermath of the Ukraine crisis, the new dynamics of global LNG market and the new supply potential for Europe emerging in areas such as the Eastern Mediterranean are just few examples of these ongoing dynamics. In this shifting context, both new challenges and new opportunities are emerging for Europe.

However, one of the key uncertainties affecting European gas markets currently relates to the future role of gas in the framework of the European decarbonisation path. An in-depth investigation of this question seems to be a fundamental prerequisite to any discussion concerning the prospects for gas in Europe. For this reason, the book devotes its first part to this controversial issue, firstly by presenting the evolution of the EU decarbonisation path from the Kyoto protocol to COP-21. This policy excursus is then followed by an analysis of the European energy markets, useful to outline all the paradoxes currently entailed in the EU decarbonisation path - such as the parallel rise of renewables and coal that Europe experienced over the last years. On the basis of this 'reality check' the potential role of gas in this process is finally assessed, both from market and policy standpoints.

The book continues by providing an insight on the future outlook of the European gas production, consumption and import requirement trends. This analysis ultimately reveals that even in the framework of strong decarbonisation scenarios the European gas import requirements will stay steady at the current level -if not even grow- over the next decades.

This figure clearly suggests that security of gas supply will continue to represent a key issue in Europe for decades to come. For this reason the second part of the book switches from the demand to the supply side, to explore a number of challenges and opportunities characterizing the European gas markets in this area. This part reviews the EU domestic gas production outlook and assesses the status of the EU-Russia gas partnership after the Ukraine crisis, before looking into the outlook for other EU traditional pipeline suppliers such as Norway, Algeria, Libya. It then continues with an analysis of the prospects for global LNG markets and their repercussions on the EU, together with an assessment of the new gas supply potential coming from the Mediterranean and the Southern Gas Corridor. Concludes this part an overview on the EU security of gas supply strategy, from its inception to its most recent developments.

The overall analysis is carried out not only from a market perspective but also from an EU policy standpoint. The adoption of such an approach seems to be indispensable for at least two reasons:

1. The European decarbonisation path has been mainly driven by the EU policy effort in the area;

2. Also due to increasing geopolitical tensions, the European institutions are today developing more and more strongly their policies in the field of security of supply.

Our aspiration is that this book might contribute to the current debate on European gas markets by providing a balancing act between decarbonisation of the European energy system and security of gas supply, two issues usually conceived as different and unmatched but in reality representing the two sides of the same coin.

Manfred Hafner and Simone Tagliapietra

1

The Demand Side: What Role for Gas in the EU Decarbonisation Path?

The EU's Quest for Decarbonisation: From Kyoto to the 20-20-20 Targets

Over the last decade, the decarbonisation of the energy system has progressively become a key priority for the European Union (EU)[1]. The first steps in this direction were taken by the EU in the framework of the international negotiations on climate change. In 2002, the EU (then still called the European Community) adopted a legislation approving the Kyoto Protocol, stating that it would jointly fulfil with its Member States[2] the commitment to reduce the collective greenhouse gas (GHG) emissions in the 2008-2012 period to 8% below 1990 levels.[3]

In this new international context, EU Member States agreed for the first time on the need for a comprehensive common action towards the increasingly challenging energy issues at the Hampton Court informal EU summit held in October 2005.[4]

Following the political momentum emerged at the summit, the European Commission (EC) published in early 2006 a Green Paper on developing a common and coherent European energy policy entitled "A European Strategy for Sustainable, Competitive and Secure Energy".[5] As the title suggests, the paper delineated a European energy policy structured on three key pillars, which continue to remain fundamental also today.

The Green Paper received the praise of the European Council of March 2006, which called for «an Energy Policy for Europe, aiming at effective Community policy, coherence between Member States and consistency between actions in different policy areas and fulfilling in a balanced way the three objectives of security of supply, competitiveness and environmental sustainability.»[6] The European Council therefore invited the EC to prepare further actions.

The Commission reacted to this endorsement by issuing in January 2007 the so-called "Energy and Climate Package", a set of measures centred on the Communication "An Energy Policy for Europe"[7] aimed at establishing a new European energy policy in line with the one proposed in the Green Paper (and thus focused on combat climate change, increase the EU' energy competitiveness and boost the EU's energy security of supply).

The European Council of March 2007 endorsed the package,[8] which was then finally adopted by the European Parliament in December 2008 after months of tough negotiations between Member States.

In addition to the definition of the triple paradigm sustainability-competitiveness-security characterizing the European energy policy, an important advancement included in the "Energy and Climate Package" was represented by the EU's commitment to reach specific targets related to GHG emissions reduction, renewable energies and energy efficiency: the well-known 20-20-20 targets. These targets encompassed a 20% reduction of GHG emissions compared to 1990, a 20% decrease of final energy demand compared to a baseline scenario and the obtainment of a level of 20% of renewable energy in total energy consumption, by 2020.

These targets had a substantial impact on the EU energy system, particularly as far as the penetration of renewable energy in the system is concerned. As Figure 1 illustrates, the share of renewable energy in the EU energy system grew substantially over the last decade, reaching a share of 15% of EU gross final energy consumption and a share of 25% of EU electricity production.

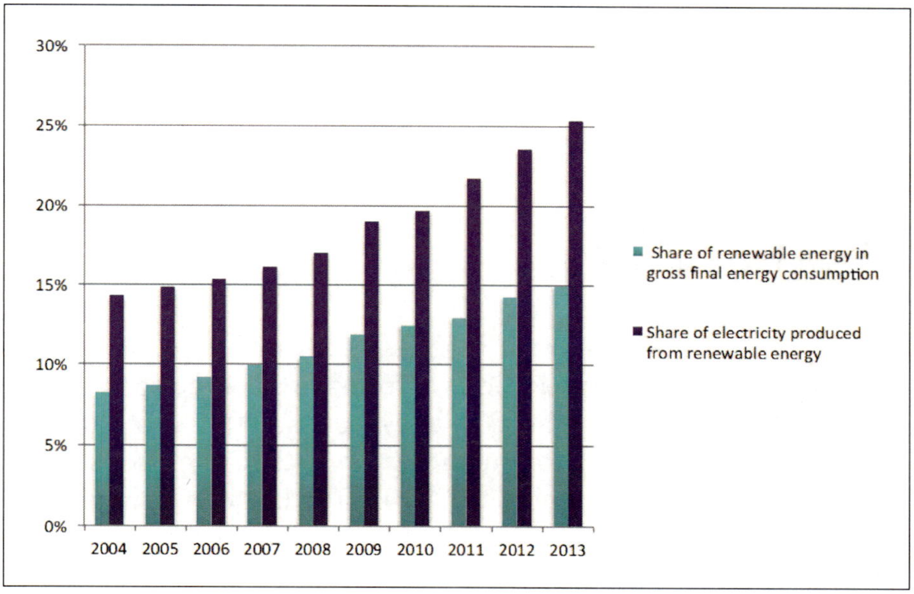

Figure 1. Share of renewable energy in the EU energy system (2004-2013).
Source: own elaboration on Eurostat (2015)[9].

The EU longer term vision of decarbonisation: the 2050 Roadmap

In March 2011 the European Council formally declared to look forward to the elaboration of a low carbon 2050 strategy providing the framework for the reduction of GHG emissions by 80-95% by 2050 compared to 1990.[10] The EU then adopted the Communication "A Roadmap for Moving to a Competitive Low Carbon Economy in 2050"[11] with the aim to outline its new long-term decarbonisation targets. The document strengthened the previous targets, to the level of envisaging a domestic GHG emissions' cut of 80% by 2050 compared to 1990 (Figure 2). Furthermore, the document reiterated the concept that the decarbonisation of the energy system is possible and could even be less costly in the long run than business-as-usual policies.

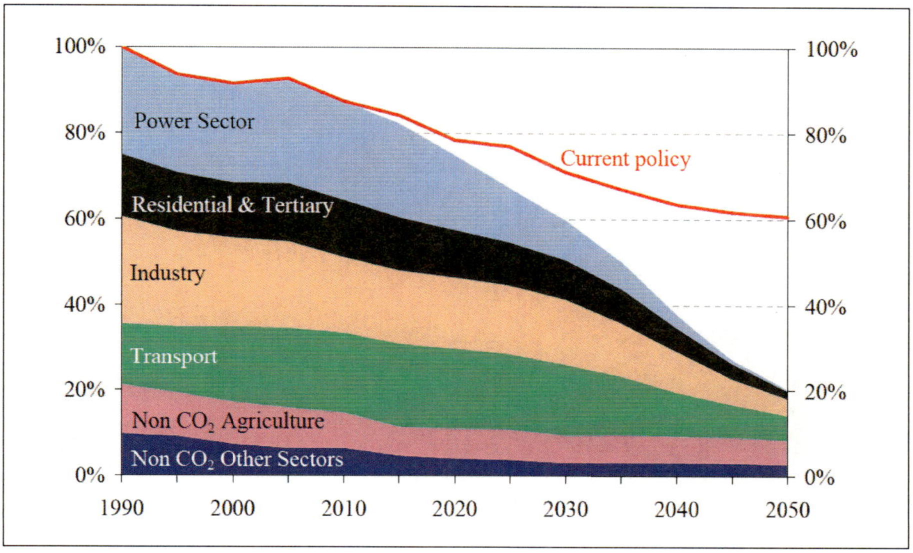

Figure 2. EU GHG emissions towards an 80% domestic reduction (100% = 1990).
Source: EC (2011a), p. 5.

In order to explore the challenges posed by delivering this decarbonisation objective while at the same time ensuring security of energy supply and competitiveness, the Commission adopted in the same year the Communication "Energy Roadmap 2050".[12] As far as natural gas is concerned, the Roadmap underlined that the fuel will be critical for the transformation of the EU energy system. According to the decarbonisation scenarios underpinning the document, natural gas will perform better than other fossil fuels and will basically maintain its 2005 share in the EU primary energy consumption up to 2050 (Figure 3).

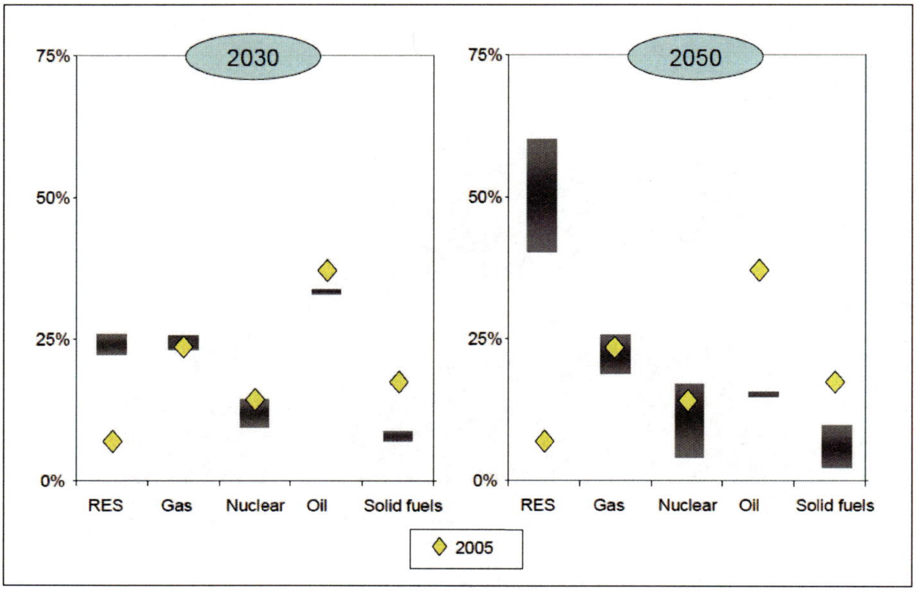

Figure 3. EU decarbonisation scenarios - 2030 and 2050 range of fuel shares in primary energy consumption compared with 2005 outcome (in %).
Source: EC (2011b), p. 5.

Towards COP-21: the 2030 Framework for Climate and Energy

In line with the two 2050 roadmaps, the EC further detailed its long-term decarbonisation strategy in 2014, with the adoption of the Communication "A Policy Framework for Climate and Energy in the Period from 2020 to 2030".[13] This new document focuses on the reduction of GHG emissions (by 40% below the 1990 levels by 2030), on the increase of renewable energy use (at least 27% of the EU's energy consumption by 2030), on the increase of energy efficiency (27% energy savings target for 2030) and on the reform of the EU Emissions Trading System (ETS).

This set of provisions was endorsed by the European Council of October 2014.[14] Following this approval, the Commission made its initial legislative proposals to implement the 2030 climate and energy framework at the end of February 2015. The proposals, set out in the "Energy Union Package".[15] aim to provide a coherent approach to climate change, energy security and competitiveness, also to achieve the goals agreed under the 2030 framework.

As previously illustrated, the EU has always been at the forefront of international efforts for climate action. This was also the case in COP-21, where the EU put a lot of effort to facilitate the reach of a new global climate deal.

In particular, following limited participation in the Kyoto Protocol and the lack of agreement in Copenhagen in 2009, the EU built a broad coalition of developed and developing countries in favor of a highly ambitious deal at COP-21. This effort ultimately contributed to shape the successful outcome of the Paris conference. The EU was the first major economy to submit its intended contribution[16] to the new agreement in March 2015.

With this document the EU and its Member States committed to a binding target of an at least 40% domestic reduction in greenhouse gas emissions by 2030 compared to 1990 levels, to be reached through the just-mentioned 2030 Framework for Climate and Energy.

The new EU targets will not be translated into national targets via EU legislation.

Considering the key importance of the new 2030 Framework not only for the EU internal policy developments but also for its global impact in relation to the agreement reached at COP-21, it is important to outline that unlike in the previous 2020 framework, the new EU targets will not be translated into national targets via EU legislation.

Officially, this is due to the willingness of leaving «greater flexibility for Member States to meet their GHG reduction targets in the most cost-effective manner in accordance with their specific circumstances, energy mixes and capacities to produce renewable energy.»[17] In reality, this seems to be mainly due to the lack of a common vision among Member States on the future trajectory of the decarbonisation path, with certain countries (from the United Kingdom to Poland) being reluctant to afford its high costs and being more sensitive to the competitiveness and security pillars of EU energy policy. This situation clearly raises questions on how the new 2030 framework will concretely be implemented.

In this uncertain situation, the role of natural gas in the EU decarbonisation path basically remains undefined, like the one of all the other components of the energy system with the notably exception of renewable energy and energy efficiency. This uncertainty opens a wide debate on the future role of natural gas in the EU energy system, particularly vis-à-vis the progressively stronger role of renewable energy in the EU energy mix.

Considering that following the decarbonisation path renewable energy will further consolidate its position of key independent variable in the EU energy equation, the next section will provide a critical assessment of the challenges and opportunities related to a major scale-up of variable renewable energy sources in the EU energy system by 2030.

Towards the achievement of the 2030 renewables target: the way ahead

According to the EC the increase of renewable energy use to 27% of overall EU energy consumption by 2030 will imply that in the same year about 45% of electricity in the EU will have to be generated by renewable energy sources.[18] This clearly represents a substantial expansion of the current contribution level of renewable energy to the EU electricity generation, estimated by Eurostat at about 25%.[19]

As illustrated in Figure 4, the EU renewable electricity generation mix still continues to be largely composed by hydro. Considering that the hydro potential in the EU is already well exploited, the new 2030 target will thus require an extensive development of variable renewable energy sources such as wind energy and solar energy (namely photovoltaic - PV -).

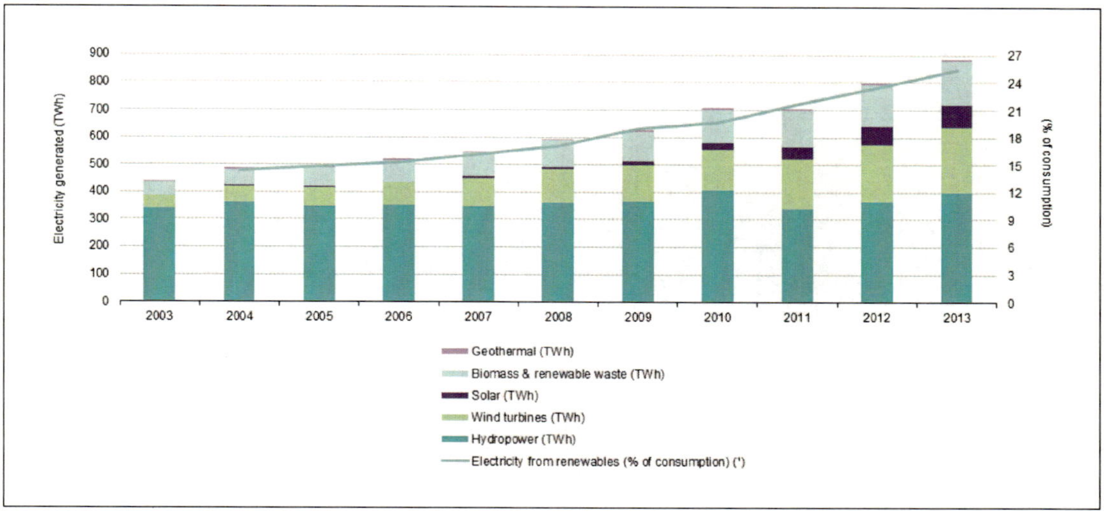

Figure 4. Electricity generated by renewable energy sources in the EU (2003-2013). Source: Eurostat (2015).

As outlined in a recent study by EDF, up to date wind and PV have been developed with a "fit and forget" logic, being not integrated into the electricity market and having priority dispatch and access to network.[20] However, a massive integration of such variable renewable energy sources into the system will require profound changes in terms of power system operation, market design, infrastructure development and transformation of conventional generation mix.

Being dependent on uncertain weather conditions, wind and PV are variable by definition and their output is both intermittent and non-dispatchable. For this reason more flexibility will be required in the system, in order to reduce this intermittency and ensure the overall stability of the system. Flexible resources include dispatchable back-up power plants, demand-side management and response, energy storage facilities and interconnections with adjacent markets.

The main tool to reduce the intermittency of wind and PV electricity generation is to aggregate their outputs over a wider geographical area. In fact, as exemplified by

Figure 5, intermittency at site level is progressively smoothed at regional, national and continental levels as a result of the diversity of outputs.

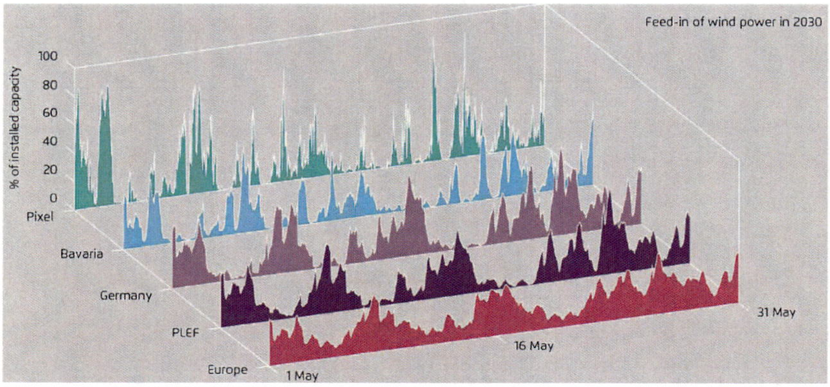

Figure 5. Time series of onshore wind power generation in a simulation for May 2030 at different levels of aggregation (as a percentage of the installed capacity at the specific aggregation level). One pixel is equivalent to an area of 2.8 x 2.8 km.
Source: Fraunhofer IWES (2015)[21]*, p. 7.*

In other words, the integration of EU electricity systems can mitigate flexibility needs arising from wind and PV, due to different weather patterns across Europe (Figure 6) that decorrelate single electricity generation peaks, yielding geographical smoothing effects that ultimately transform intermittency at local level in variability at EU level.

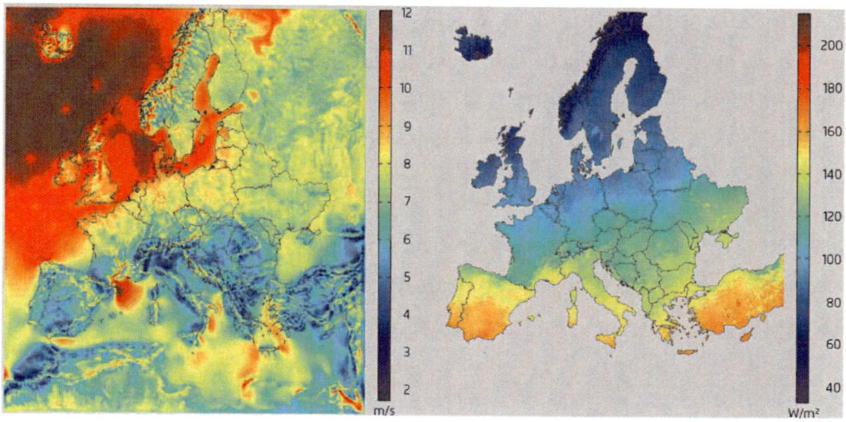

Figure 6. Wind and solar resource throughout Europe for the year 2007. Average wind speed approx. 70 m above the ground (left) and average global horizontal irradiation (right). Source: Fraunhofer IWES (2015), p. 21.

In addition to this, a strong integration of EU electricity systems can allow the cross-border exchanges necessary to minimise surplus renewable electricity generation. As outlined by Fraunhofer IWES, «when no trading options exist, hours with high domestic wind and PV generation require that generation from renewables be stored or curtailed in part. With market integration, decorrelated production peaks across countries enable exports to regions where the load is not covered. By contrast, a hypothetical national autarchy case has storage or curtailment requirements that are ten times as high.»[22]

The process of integration of EU electricity systems will require the development of an appropriate network infrastructure, and particularly of interconnections not only able to transport wind and PV electricity production to consuming centres but also to share thermal generation capacity between EU countries.

The development of an appropriate infrastructure is thus not only crucial to reduce variability of wind and PV at system level but also to reduce the overall need for back-up electricity generation. This represents a vital element, particularly if considering that by displacing baseload generation (i.e. from conventional sources) wind and PV do increase the need for back-up capacity.[23]

With an increased role of wind and PV in EU electricity systems, conventional plants are thus progressively switching from their traditional roles to a new back-up role, essential to guarantee the stability of the overall system vis-à-vis the variability of wind and PV.

In addition to interconnections, flexibility in the system could theoretically be enhanced with demand side management and demand response mechanisms as well as energy storage. However, these solutions face major challenges. Demand mechanisms are partially challenged by socio-economic issues such as consumer behavioural changes, albeit can well be implemented in the industry and services sectors first. Energy storage is challenged by a persistent technological gap; in fact, to date

Conventional sources will continue to play a key role in guaranteeing system stability and security of supply.

the only operative option is represented by pumped storage hydropower, as other technologies such as battery systems, compressed air energy storage, flywheels and hydrogen storage continue to be highly expensive. In sum, in the medium-term these solutions will unlikely provide a substantial contribution for back-up in the system.

In this framework, exploiting the complementary roles of renewable and conventional electricity generation sources will be even more important in the future EU electricity systems. In particular, conventional sources will continue to play a key role in guaranteeing system stability and security of supply by being able to provide larger and more rapid increases and decreases in output in order to accommodate increasing amounts of variable renewables-based generation.

With regard to this specific aspect, the International Energy Agency (IEA) points out that «the integration of high levels of wind and PV into electricity systems may require market framework reforms to guarantee a sufficient level of investment in the conventional power plants needed to keep the system in balance, together with other measures to shift demand when sun is not shining or the wind is not blowing. Failing to address these needs in advance will negatively impact the reliability of the electricity system.»[24]

On the basis of the situation illustrated in this section, this seems to be particularly urgent in the case of the EU, where variable renewables are set to become the cornerstone of the electricity system, increasing the variability that the rest of the system has to manage. Of course, a new EU electricity market design should also be able to provide adequate economic incentive for investments in the previously mentioned flexibility options (i.e. network infrastructure expansion, development of smart grids, adoption of demand side measures and development of energy storage technologies), crucial to ensure the sustainability of the EU decarbonisation path also beyond the 2030 horizon.

To make a long story short, in order to achieve its 2030 renewable energy target the EU will need to rethink its electricity system beyond renewable energy itself. The role of conventional fuels in the future system should be better investigated, also to provide investors with the minimum grade of certainty needed to make today investments that will define the EU electricity system of 2030 and beyond. This is particularly true considering the recent, controversial, evolution of the EU electricity generation mix, which will be described in the next section.

The EU decarbonisation path and the (unwelcome) renaissance of coal

As the previous sections illustrated, over the last decade the EU has successfully promoted the expansion of renewable energy sources in the European electricity generation mix. However, part of the environmental benefits generated by this complex and costly expansion has been nullified by the parallel growth of coal in the mix, a trend particularly emerged after 2010 (Figure 7).

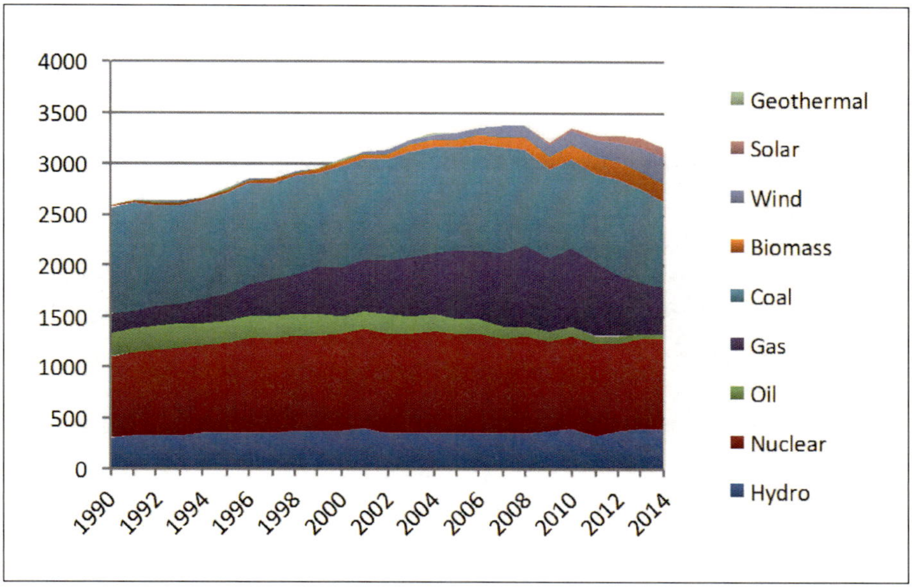

Figure 7. Electricity production in the EU by source 1990-2014 (TWh)
Source: own elaboration on Enerdata (2016).

The key driver underpinning this trend was the US shale gas revolution. In fact, as US utilities progressively shifted into natural gas, American coal miners had to look for new markets abroad.

In the meantime, many new large mining capacities that were committed in Indonesia and Australia during the boom period of Asian demand (2008-2011) progressively came online between 2012 and 2014, adding even more low-cost supply to the international coal market. Considering that in the meantime coal demand growth in Asia resulted to be lower than expected, the global coal market entered a situation of over-supply.

As a result of this trend, overall EU coal imports increased from 104 million tons of oil equivalent (Mtoe) in 2010 to 119 Mtoe in 2014 and coal import prices plunged from EUR 130 per tonne (t) in March 2008 to below EUR 60 per t in May 2014 at the

EU import reference price.[25] Due to a progressive transition from oil indexation to spot pricing, natural gas prices in the EU also decreased over the last years, but at a far slower pace than coal. In this framework, coal became more competitive against natural gas in the EU electricity generation sector. This led to a significant gas-to-coal switch in the EU, mainly in the United Kingdom, Spain and Germany, but also in the Netherlands.

Considering that coal-fired electricity generation emits more CO_2 per kWh than other power plants, this situation represents a substantial challenge to the EU decarbonisation path. This is particularly true if considering that the efficiency of the EU's coal-fired power plants fleet is on average low, with a level of 36% compared to the one of 45% characterizing the most efficient plants, such as the ultra-super critical power plants in Germany.[26]

The existing EU environmental regulation has not had a relevant impact on the cost-advantage that coal-fired generators have enjoyed over their competitors. In fact, according to the IEA, the EU Large Combustion Plant Directive (LCPD)[27] «is expected to lead to retiring 8 GW of coal-fired power capacity in the United Kingdom. In other EU countries, reductions are expected to be much lower, totaling around 10 GW. All in all, the shutdowns would affect around 2% of EU total generating capacity.»[28]

In short, a global market over-supply combined with a lack of proper environmental regulation at the EU level, allowed coal to stage a renaissance in EU electricity market over the last few years.

Global market over-supply and lack of regulation allowed a coal renaissance in EU electricity market.

In this context, natural gas found itself in the uncomfortable position to be squeezed by subsidised renewable energy sources on one side and cheap coal on the other side. This added additional pressure to the already weak natural gas demand conditions in the EU (due to the economic crisis and mild winters), resulting in a dramatic plunge of EU natural gas demand from a peak level of 505 billion cubic metres (bcm) in 2010 to a level of 394 bcm in 2014: the same level recorded in 1995[29] (Figure 8).

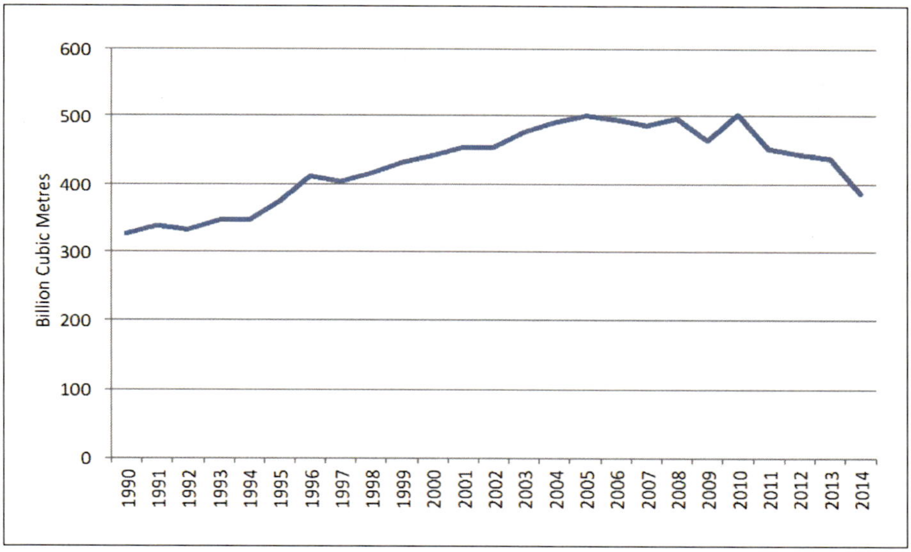

Figure 8. EU natural gas demand (1990-2014). Source: own elaboration on BP (2015).

At a first view, this graph might suggest that the role of natural gas in the EU energy system is irreversibly in decline, particularly if taking into consideration the EU's quest to further advance renewable energy in electricity generation. However, considering that the previous analysis clearly illustrated that a strong expansion of renewable energy by 2030 and beyond will not exclude a key role of conventional electricity generation in the system, the future role of natural gas in the EU decarbonisation path does deserve to be better explored.

Exploring the future role of gas in the EU decarbonisation path

Albeit technically feasible, a further large-scale development of wind and PV in the EU electricity system might potentially encounter economic barriers due to increasing system integration costs. This issue is particularly relevant if considering that the EU itself acknowledges «that in the future, the benefits of renewable energy must be exploited in a way which is to the greatest extent possible market driven»[30] and thus not based on support schemes that ultimately hinder market integration and reduce cost-efficiency.

In this context, assessing the future role of conventional electricity generation is of vital importance for the stability and security of the EU electricity system. As an overall trend, considering the previously illustrated characteristics of an electricity system centred on variable renewable energy sources, what will be needed is primarily a park of flexible power plants, where flexibility of a power plant is defined as its ability to run in partial load as well as by parameters such as ramping rates, start-up time and minimum down time.[31]

Among the various possible options of conventional electricity generation (natural gas, coal, nuclear and oil), natural gas seems to be the fuel better placed to play a key complementary role to wind and PV in the decarbonisation path for the following four reasons:

1. First of all, natural gas-fired power plants can provide the flexible back-up capacity needed in a system with high share of variable renewable energy sources. An analysis carried out by Eurelectric (see Figure 9) shows that among conventional electricity generation technologies pumped storage is the most responsive one, as it can be called upon to generate electricity almost instantaneously and as it can ramp up and down by more than 40% of the nominal output per minute. However, being contingent to specific geographical conditions, pumped storage cannot provide the flexible back-up capacity needed at system level. Among other technologies, combined-cycle gas turbines (CCGTs) are particularly suitable for load-following operation as they have both fast load gradients (4%/min) and can be brought online fairly quickly (less then 1.5 hours from warm conditions). These performances are far beyond those of coal-fired power plants (which are less responsive than any other technologies) and of nuclear power plants (which cannot be brought online from cold and warm conditions in timeframes similar to those of other technologies). For this reason natural gas-fired power plants can well play an important role in meeting the flexibility challenge arising from variable renewable energy sources.[32]

	NPP	HC	LIGN	CCG	PS
Start-up Time "cold"	~ 40H	~ 6H	~ 10H	< 2H	~ 0,1H
Start-up Time "warm"	~ 40H	~ 3H	~ 6H	< 1,5H	~ 0,1H
Load Gradient ↗ "nominal Output"	~ 5%/M	~ 2%/M	~ 2%/M	~ 4%/M	> 40%/M
Load Gradient ↘ "nominal Output"	~ 5%/M	~ 2%/M	~ 2%/M	~ 4%/M	> 40%/M
Minimal Shutdown Time	←	NO		→	~ 10H
Minimal possible Load	50%	40%	40%	<50%	~ 15%

Figure 9. Flexibility of conventional electricity generation technologies. Note: NPP: nuclear power plants; HC: hard-coal fired power plants; Lign: lignite-fired power plants; CCG: combined cycle gas-fired power plants; PS: pumped storage power plants.
Source: Eurelectric (2011), p. 19.

2. By displacing coal in the EU electricity generation systems natural gas has the potential to generate immediate and substantial GHG emissions' reductions. In fact, modern CCGTs produce about half the CO_2 emissions per unit of electricity generated compared with coal-fired plants.[33] Considering that coal still plays a key role in the EU electricity system (see Figure 10) the scale of this switch might provide a consistent contribution to the EU 2030 GHG emissions reduction target.

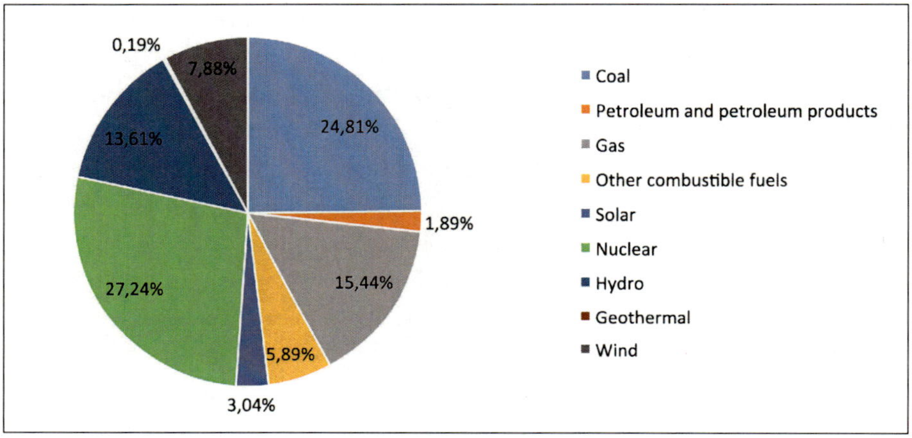

Figure 10. EU electricity generation by source, 2013.
Source: own elaboration on Eurostat (2016).

3. A switch from coal-fired power plants to natural gas-fired power plants will not only positively impact the EU environmental effort at macro level (i.e. climate change mitigation) but also at micro level. In fact, as the IEA outlines, «compared with coal and oil, natural gas avoids or reduces much of the local environmental damage arising from fossil-fuel use. Gas gives off fewer pollutants when burned, including the nitrogen oxide (NO_x) that contributes to acidification and ground-level ozone formation; the sulphur dioxide (SO_2) that (with NO_x) causes acid rain; and the particulate matter that (again with NO_x) causes smog and poor air quality. Consequently, using natural gas instead of other fossil fuels in electricity generation (and other sectors) offers the opportunity to improve air quality, especially in and around cities, where this problem is most acute.»[34]

4. Being the second-largest emitter of CO_2 after the electricity generation sector (Figure 11), the transport sector has an important role to play in the EU decarbonisation path.

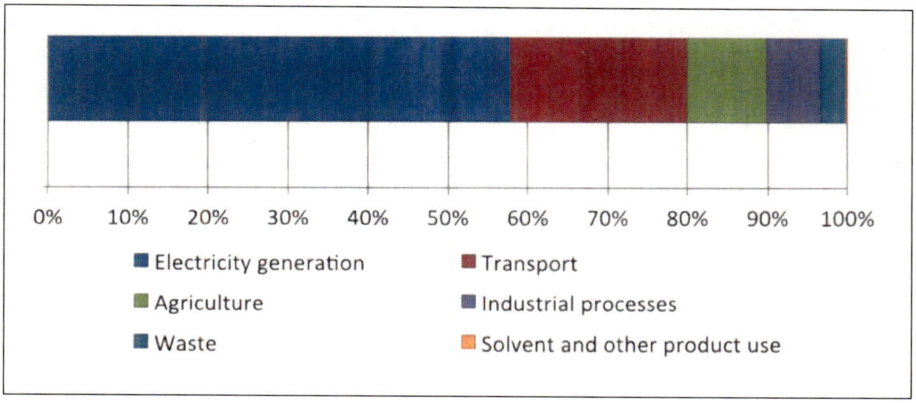

Figure 11. GHG emissions in the EU by sector, 2013.
Source: own elaboration on Eurostat (2016).

GHG emissions from the transport sector decreased since 2007 due to high oil prices, increased efficiency of passengers' cars and slower growth in mobility. The EC[35] expects this trend to continue but this will still not be sufficient to meet the goal to reduce GHG emissions from the sector by 60% by 2050 compared to 1990 and by 20% by 2030 compared to emissions in 2008 as set by the Transport White Paper[36] adopted in 2011.

Notwithstanding their current difficulties (e.g. relatively high costs, low energy density of batteries and lack of recharging infrastructure), electric vehicles will most likely play a key role in the future decarbonisation of the transport sector. However, natural gas can also play a role in the field, not only in terms of compressed natural gas (CNG) vehicles, but particularly in terms of liquefied natural gas (LNG) for trucks and for ships.

For instance, ExxonMobil does not expect a significant growth in natural gas as a transportation fuel for light-duty vehicles (as CNG vehicles cost more than comparable gasoline-powered cars, have a shorter driving range due to CNG's lower energy intensity, and challenging remains the development of a large network of easily accessible refueling stations) but it does expect a significant development in terms of LNG for trucks, as LNG-fuelled long-haul trucks have the capacity to travel up to 1,200 km between fill-ups while pulling heavy loads and fuel cost savings could recoup the higher investment costs for an LNG truck (US$70,000 to US$90,000 compared to diesel) within about three years.[37] The same rationale also applies to LNG-fuelled buses.

Furthermore, LNG is also expected to play an important role as a ship fuel. According to DNV GL, the world's largest classification society, 63 LNG-fuelled ships (excluding LNG carriers) already operate worldwide, while another 76 are on order (as of May 2015).[38] The key driver behind the choice of LNG as ship fuel relates to its environmental advantages. In fact, ships are generally fuelled by highly polluting fuels such as heavy fuel oil, marine gas oil or distillate fuels. The utilization of LNG allows to significantly reduce local pollution, and thus to safeguard the ecosystems on which ships are operating. This is the reason why the use of LNG as a ship fuel is increasingly encouraged by the authorities of major European harbours, from Rotterdam to Hamburg, from Antwerp to Bremerhaven.[39]

LNG is expected to play an important role as a ship fuel.

Along the same lines, a recent study published by the Oxford Institute for Energy Studies on the prospects of natural gas in the transport sector also concludes that «the answer to the question on whether natural gas is a realistic fuelling alternative [in transport] is yes for heavy trucks and marine, possibly for buses with the case for passenger cars being hardest to make.»[40]

Towards a more balanced and secure decarbonisation path

As illustrated in the paper, over the last decade the EU has made consistent progress towards the decarbonisation of its energy system. However, this process has also brought new challenges to the EU energy markets, generating certain paradoxes (such as the parallel growth of renewable energy and coal in the mix) that need to be addressed in order to ensure the sustainability of the EU decarbonisation path.

Considering that after the first rump-up phase - occurred over the last decade - the future integration of more variable renewable energy sources into the system will be more complex both under the technical and economic perspectives, the EU decarbonisation path should indeed now find a more balanced and secure trajectory. In particular, a new EU electricity market design should be able to provide adequate economic incentive for investments in the flexibility options (i.e. network infrastructure expansion, development of smart grids, adoption of demand side measures and development of energy storage technologies) that will be crucial to ensure the sustainability of the EU decarbonisation path also beyond the 2030 horizon.

As the paper illustrated, in order to achieve its 2030 renewable energy target the EU will need to rethink its electricity system beyond renewable energy itself, with a particular focus on the role that natural gas might play in the future of the EU energy system.

1 - The Demand Side

Considering its previously illustrated characteristics, and particularly taking into consideration the potential to generate immediate and substantial GHG emissions' reductions by displacing coal with it, natural gas might well play an important role in the future EU decarbonisation path. Its role does not need to be supported by dedicated public policies but, on the contrary, what is needed is a more general EU action aimed at rebalancing the overall energy system along the lines of a truly sustainable decarbonisation path.

Such an action should be carried out by making use of two specific tools: 1. Carbon pricing; 2. Environmental regulation.

1. Speeding-up the reform of the Emissions Trading Scheme (ETS)

The development of a well-functioning (and technology-neutral) carbon pricing system, able to discourage high carbon options and to promote most cost-efficient ways of reducing GHG emissions, is theoretically the essential component of a sustainable decarbonisation path.

In fact, this system would create the basis of an automatic readjustment of EU electricity markets ideally composed by a progressive phase out of highly polluting coal-fired power plants, a strong development of renewable energy sources (even in absence of incentives) and a larger utilization of natural gas in electricity generation.

In 2005 the EU adopted the Emission Trading Scheme (ETS) as its flagship GHG emissions' reduction initiative. The scheme, based on the "cap and trade" principle, aims at providing appropriate incentives for investments in low-carbon technology via a carbon emissions price.[41] After two initial phases.[42] the ETS entered its third trading phase at the beginning of 2013, with the introduction of a EU-wide cap on emissions (reduced by 1.74% each year) and a progressive shift towards auctioning of emission allowances (EUAs) in place of cost-free allocation. However, low levels of industrial output and power generation due to the economic crisis have resulted in an increasingly large surplus of EUAs in the ETS, leading to a significant downward pressure on the carbon emissions price (Figure 12).

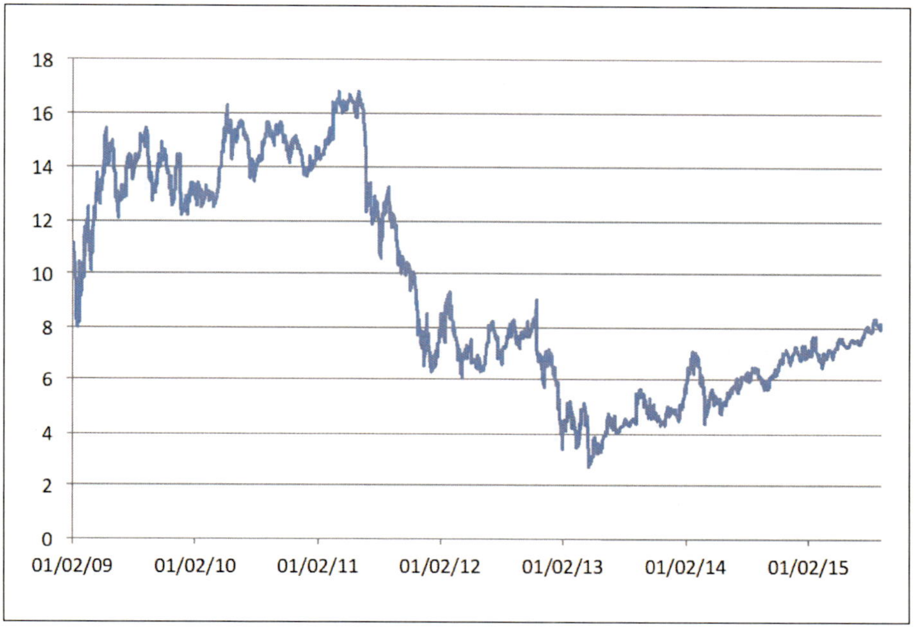

Figure 12. EU ETS carbon emissions spot price, EUR per tonne.
Source: own elaboration on European Energy Exchange (2015).

Considering the current inability of the ETS to send sufficient price signals to investors in low-carbon technologies, with the 2030 Climate and Energy Framework the EC has brought forward proposals to address the level of over-supply in the ETS and reintroduce a meaningful carbon emissions price.[43] This reform should be seen as the crucial element towards the consolidation of the EU decarbonisation path and, consequently, of the creation of a more balanced EU energy system on which renewables develop in parallel to other low-carbon and flexible solutions, such as natural gas.

2. Tightening environmental regulation

Considering the numerous challenges related to the development of a well-functioning carbon pricing system at the EU level, the instrument of environmental regulation should also be exploited to rebalance the energy system along the lines of a sustainable decarbonisation path. In particular, tighter emission performance standards should be applied to power plants.

In 2011 the Industrial Emissions Directive (IED)[44] came into force, updating and merging seven pieces of existing legislation, including the previously illustrated Large Combustion Plant Directive (LCPD). The new IED places further restrictions on the level of nitrogen oxides, sulphur dioxide and particulate emissions permitted from power generators after 1 January 2016 (as until the end of 2015 the provisions of LDPD are applied).[45]

It is difficult to envisage whether these provisions will have or not a consistent impact on the European coal-fired power plants fleet. This will largely depend on the materialization of the incentive to invest in depollution equipment, a choice set to be driven by technology cost and coal pricing itself. According to Cedigaz (2014), for old coal-fired power plants there will be no incentive to invest in depollution equipment and 50-55 GW of EU coal power capacity may thus close by 2020/2023 at the latest according to the IED.[46] However, other analyses carried out by European climate think-tanks suggest that a predominant share of EU coal power plants will become IED compliant, as technological changes and flexibility in IED rules will make compliance much less costly than previously estimated.[47]

The implementation of the IED should thus be followed closely, also through the system of review already adopted by the EC. At the same time, the EU should be ready to take further actions on environmental regulation, in order to ensure the achievement of proper environmental standards in the EU power plants fleet.

Carbon pricing and environmental regulation constitute the optimal tool-set to calibrate the energy system along the lines of a sustainable decarbonisation path. If correctly utilized, these tools could stimulate a further development of renewable energy sources, a greater role of natural gas in the energy mix and a reduction in the utilization of polluting coal, at one fell swoop. This readjustment seems to be the only way to make decarbonisation balanced and secure up to 2030 and beyond.

Notes

1 This part is based on: M. Hafner, S. Tagliapietra (2015), *The Role of Natural Gas in the EU Decarbonisation Path,* Nota di Lavoro n. 86.2015, Fondazione Eni Enrico Mattei, Milano.

2 15 at the time: Austria, Belgium, Denmark, Finland, France, Germany, Greece, Ireland, Italy, Luxembourg, Netherlands, Portugal, Spain, Sweden and the United Kingdom.

3 European Council (2002), *Decision Concerning the Approval, on Behalf of the European Community, of the Kyoto Protocol to the United Nations Framework Convention on Climate Change and the Joint Fulfilment of Commitments Thereunder,* 2002/358/EC, 25 April.

4 During the summit the EU heads of State or Government discussed a plan presented by the British Prime Minister to create a true European energy policy and agreed on the need of advancing the EU action in this field. See: i) Tony Blair (2005), *Press Conference at EU Informal Summit Hampton Court,* 27 October; ii) Dieter Helm (2005), *European Energy Policy: Securing Supplies and Meeting the Challenge of Climate Change,* Paper prepared for the UK Presidency of the EU; iii) EurActiv (2005), Blair Calls for Stronger EU Energy Policy Co-operation, 31 October.

5 European Commission (2006), *A European Strategy for Sustainable, Competitive and Secure Energy,* Green Paper of the Commission, COM(2006) 105 final.

6 European Council (2006), *Presidency Conclusions,* No 7775/1/06 REV1, 24 March.

7 European Commission (2007), *An Energy Policy for Europe,* Communication from the Commission to the European Council and the European Parliament, COM(2007) 1 final.

8 European Council (2007), *Presidency Conclusions,* No 7224/07, 9 March.

9 Eurostat (2015), SHARES 2013 - *Short Assessment of Renewable Energy Sources,* available at: http://ec.europa.eu/eurostat/web/energy/data/shares

10 European Council (2011), *Conclusions,* 4 February 2011, EUCO 2/1/11.

11 European Commission (2011a), *A Roadmap for Moving to a Competitive Low Carbon Economy in 2050,* Communication from the Commission to the European Parliament, the Council, the Economic and Social Committee and the Committee on the Regions, COM(2011) 112 final.

12 European Commission (2011b) *Energy Roadmap 2050,* Communication from the Commission to the European Parliament, the Council, the European Economic and Social Committee and the Committee on the Regions, COM(2011) 885 final.

13 European Commission (2014), *A Policy Framework for Climate and Energy in the Period from 2020 to 2030,* Communication from the Commission to the European Parliament, the Council, the European Economic and Social Committee and the Committee on the Regions, COM(2014) 15, final.

14 European Council (2014), *Conclusions on 2030 Climate and Energy Policy Framework,* SN 79/14, 24 October.

15 The package is composed by three Communications: i) European Commission (2015a), *A Framework Strategy for a Resilient Energy Union with a Forward-Looking Climate Change Policy,* COM(2015) 80 final; European Commission

(2015b), *The Paris Protocol - A blueprint for tackling global climate change beyond 2020,* COM(2015) 81 final; European Commission (2015c), *Achieving the 10% electricity interconnection target - Making Europe's electricity grid fit for 2020,* COM(2015) 82 final.

16 Latvian Presidency of the Council of the European Union (2015), *Submission by Latvia and the European Commission on Behalf of the European Union and Its Member States - Subject: Intended Nationally Determined Contribution of the EU and its Member States,* Riga, 6 March 2015.

17 European Commission (2014), Op. Cit., p. 6. This attitude reflects the traditional reluctance of Member States to give up to the EU any competence concerning the composition of their own energy mixes. It also underpins the provisions on energy of the Treaty of Lisbon, contained in Article 194 TFUE. See: Official Journal of the European Union (2008), *Consolidated versions of the Treaty on European Union (TEU) and the Treaty on the Functioning of the European Union* (TFEU), OJ 2008/C 115.

18 European Commission (2014), *Op. Cit.,* p. 6.

19 Eurostat (2015), *Op. Cit.,* data refers to 2013.

20 EDF (2015), *Technical and Economic Analysis of the European Electricity System with 60% RES, Research and Development Division,* 17 June 2015.

21 Fraunhofer IWES (2015), *The European Power System in 2030: Flexibility Challenges and Integration Benefits. An Analysis with a Focus on the Pentalateral Energy Forum Region, Analysis on behalf of Agora Energiewende.*

22 *Ibidem,* p. 1.

23 In fact, generation from wind and PV contributes to the supply of energy but their stochastic nature means that their outputs do not always coincide with periods of high demand and consequently they make a minor contribution to capacity.

24 IEA (2015), *Energy and Climate Change,* World Energy Outlook Special Report, Paris, p. 112.

25 IEA (2014), *Op. Cit.,* p. 226.

26 IEA (2014), *Op. Cit.,* p. 224.

27 Official Journal (2001), *Directive 2001/80/EC of the European Parliament and of the Council of 23 October 2001 on the Limitation of Emissions of Certain Pollutants Into the Air From Large Combustion Plants,* L 309, Vol. 44, 27 November 2011. The Directive aims at reducing acidification, ground level ozone and particulates by controlling the emissions of sulphur dioxide, oxides of nitrogen and dust from large combustion plants. All combustion plants built after 1987 must comply with the LCPD emission limits. Those power stations in operation before 1987 have three options for complying: 1) by installing emission abatement equipment, e.g. flue-gas desulphurisation; 2) by operating within a "National Plan" setting a national annual mass of emissions calculated by applying the emission limit value (ELV) approach to existing plants, on the basis of those plants' average actual operating hours, fuel used and thermal input, over the five years to 2000; or 3) by opting out of the directive. An existing plant that chooses to opt out is restricted to 20,000 total hours of operation after 2007 and must close by the end of 2015.

Notes

28 IEA (2014), *Op. Cit.*, p. 224.

29 BP (2015), *BP Statistical Review of World Energy 2015*, London.

30 European Commission (2014), *Op. Cit.*, p. 6.

31 In all thermal power plants partial load operation is restricted by a minimum power generation.

32 For the complete analysis please refer to: Eurelectric (2011), *Flexible Generation: Backing-Up Renewables*, Brussels.

33 IEA (2011), *Are We Entering a Golden Age of Gas?*, World Energy Outlook Special Report, Paris, p. 85

34 *Ibidem*, p. 85.

35 European Commission (2014), Op. Cit., p. 14.

36 European Commission (2011), *White Paper - Roadmap to a Single European Transport Area. Towards a Competitive and Resource Efficient Transport System*, COM(2011) 144, final.

37 ExxonMobil official website: http://corporate.exxonmobil.com/en/energy/natural-gas/technology/natural-gas-as-a-transportation-fuel?parentId=7bb4486e-b68e-43ee-b9fa-cff1663bd80c

38 DVN GL (2015), *LNG as a Ship Fuel*, Hamburg.

39 Reuters (2014), *Global Transport Sector Looks to Ride Natural Gas Boom*, February 5.

40 Chris Le Fevre (2014), *The Prospects for Natural Gas as a Transport Fuel in Europe*, NG84, Oxford Institute for Energy Studies, Oxford.

41 Specifically, the scheme works as follow: the overall volume of GHG that can be emitted each year by the power plants, factories and other companies covered by the system is subject to a cap set at EU level. Within this Europe-wide cap, companies receive or buy emission allowances, which they can trade if they wish. For a detailed overview please refer to: European Commission (2013), *The EU Emission Trading System (EU ETS)*, Climate Action Publications.

42 [illegible]hase, 2005-2007: trading period used for "learning by doing". EU ETS established as the world's biggest carbon [illegible]arket. However, the number of allowances, based on estimated needs, turns out to be excessive; consequently the price of first-period allowances falls to zero in 2007. 2nd Phase, 2008-2012: the number of allowances is reduced by 6.5% for the period, but the economic downturn cuts emissions, and thus demand, by even more. This leads to a surplus of unused allowances and credits, which weighs on carbon price. See: European Commission (2013), *Op. Cit.*

43 According to the Commission (2014, *Op. Cit.*, p. 8), «the best way to achieve this is to establish a market stability reserve at the start of phase 4 trading in 2021. The market stability reserve would provide an automatic adjustment of the supply of auctioned allowances downwards or upwards based on a pre-defined set of rules and would improve resilience to market shocks and enhance market stability.»

44 Official Journal (2010), *Directive 2010/75/EU of the European Parliament and of the Council of 24 November 2010 on Industrial Emissions (Integrated Pollution Prevention and Control)*, L 334, 17.12.2010.

45 In particular, in comparison with the previous LCPD the new IED tightens emission limit values (ELVs) for sulphur dioxide from a level of 400 milligrams per cubic metre (mg/Nm3) to a level of 200 mg/Nm3. Furthermore, power generators will

have to install selective catalytic reduction from 2016 to meet the nitrogen oxides ELVs. Peaking plants (<1,500 annual operating hours) can run indefinitely, a Transitional National Plan to mid-2020 allows trading in most pollutant categories to achieve emissions reductions equivalent to the Directive's ELVs, and a derogation allows operators to run their plants for just 17,500 hours after 1 January 2016 before closure, which must be before the end of 2023.

46 Cedigaz (2014), *Gas and Coal Competition in the EU Power Sector,* Rueil Malmaison.

47 In particular, Sandbag (a UK-based climate think-tank) estimates that across the EU 110 out of 150 GW are or will become IED compliant. The remaining 40 GW could become compliant too if it invests in NO_x abatement. According to the analysis, it had been thought that the only way to comply would be to install selective catalytic reduction that turns NO_x into nitrogen and water. However, cheaper options such as selective non-catalytic reduction have become available in the meantime. See: Sandbag (2014), *Europe's Failure to Tackle Coal - Risks for the EU Low Carbon Transition,* London.

2

The Supply Side: New Challenges and Opportunities ahead

The EU domestic gas production outlook and the rise of import requirements

The EU domestic gas production has dramatically fallen since the early 2000s, sliding from a level of 235 Bcm in 2001 to a level of 132 Bcm in 2014. This trend has been predominantly driven by the United Kingdom, where production collapsed from 108 Bcm in 2000 to 37 Bcm in 2014. However, more recently the Netherlands has also provided a contribution to the fall, by reducing its production from 70 Bcm in 2010 to 56 Bcm in 2014 (see Figure 13).

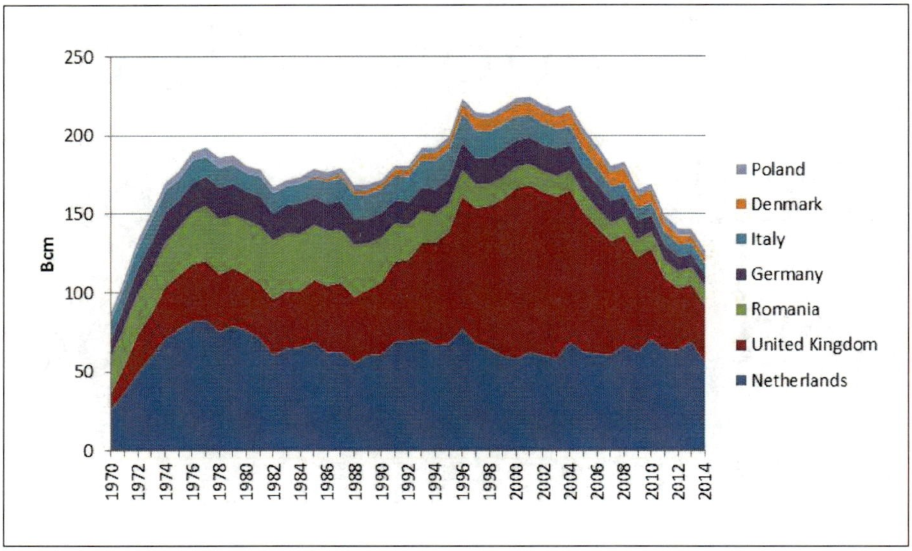

Figure 13. Evolution of key European gas producers (1970-2014).
Source: authors' elaboration on BP (2015).

This decline, mainly driven by rapidly depleting resources throughout the EU, will most likely continue in the future.

In the Netherlands, currently the EU's largest gas producer, the government decided in early 2014 to cap the production at the large Groningen gas field following earthquakes in the production region. Limits on Groningen production were initially set at 42.5 Bcm for 2015 and 2016, and at 40 Bcm for 2016[1]. However, in December 2015 the government ultimately decided to further limit the extraction at Groningen, to a level of 27 Bcm for the 2015/2016 gas year.[2] While taking this decision, the government also outlined its intention to further reduce long-term production levels at the gas field, possibly to a level between 18 and 24 Bcm in 2020.[3] In this framework, a further gas production decline in the Netherlands will be unavoidable in coming years. Furthermore, it should be outlined that Groningen has always played a very important role of swing producer in continental North-western Europe. The reduced future output of the field could thus put into question this role, therefore reducing the overall flexibility of European gas markets. Considering the expected future strong demand for flexibility generated by the high penetration of renewables into the European systems, this might create new challenges which can only partially be addressed by the increased flexibility provided by eventual additional LNG imports. In the United Kingdom the declining gas production trend is also set to continue. Government's scenarios illustrate that production will decline further in the 2020s, to reach about 20 Bcm in 2030.[4] It should be noted that a significant share of future gas production is expected to come from new fields. Considering the current low oil and gas prices environment, investing in the development of these new fields might well turn out to be challenging for oil and gas companies. This might add further uncertainty to the future outlook of gas production in the United Kingdom.

Over the last few years expectations have emerged in the EU about the opportunity of rebalancing the declining conventional gas production story with a new, potential, unconventional gas production narrative.[5] However, these expectations have soon proved to be illusory, due to disappointing test wells, regulatory constraints, and continued public hostility. Moratoria forbidding unconventional gas extraction were adopted in different countries both de jure (e.g. France, Bulgaria, the Netherlands)

Over the next decades the EU domestic gas production will continue its downwards trajectory.

and de facto (e.g. Germany). These constrains have added to deteriorating economics as a result of lower oil and gas prices that have all contributed to dimming the outlook for unconventional gas in the EU, even in the case of the one regarded as the most promising unconventional gas hotspot in the EU: Poland. In this country eight of the eleven international oil and gas companies which had invested in the sector indeed halted their exploration activities by end-2015.[6]

In sum, over the next decades the EU domestic gas production will thus continue its downwards trajectory. In this framework the EU import requirements will consistently rise with respect to the current level - independently from the evolution of the EU gas demand. The best way to illustrate this trend is to have a look at the latest (2015) three key scenarios developed by the International Energy Agency (IEA)[7]:

1. The Current Policies Scenario, where no changes from current policies are assumed;

2. The New Policies Scenario, where broad policy commitments and plans that have been announced by countries, including national pledges to reduce greenhouse-gas emissions and plans to phase out fossil-energy subsidies, are considered;

3. The 450 Scenario, which sets out an energy pathway consistent with the goal of limiting the global increase in temperature to 2°C by limiting concentration of greenhouse gases in the atmosphere to around 450 parts per million of CO_2.

As shown in Figure 14, the EU gas demand outlook changes significantly in the three scenarios, up to a differential of 200 Bcm in the 2040 projections of the Current Policies Scenario and the 450 Scenario. Notwithstanding the wide diversity of these demand scenarios, the EU import requirements grow in all the cases with respect to the current level, due to production trends - declining in all scenarios.

The EU domestic gas production outlook and the rise of import requirements

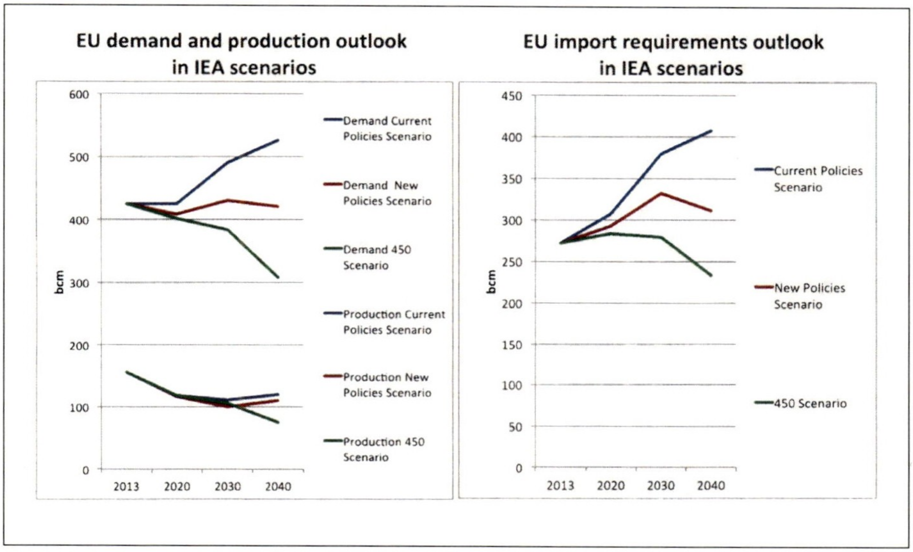

Figure 14. Source: authors' elaboration on IEA (2015).

The highest rise in EU gas import requirements is, of course, expected in the Current Policies Scenario, with an increase of 35 Bcm in 2020, 108 Bcm in 2030 and 136 Bcm in 2040 with respect to the import requirement level of 2013. Even in the strongest decarbonisation scenario, the 450 Scenario, import requirements rise over the next decades, by 12 Bcm in 2020 and 7 Bcm in 2030 to decline only in 2040 by 38 Bcm with respect to the 2013 level.

The rising level of gas import requirements illustrated in these scenarios unveil the structural nature of the EU dependency on external gas suppliers. This element, combined with the limited composition of gas import portfolio illustrated in Figure 15, outlines the importance of the security of gas supply issue in the EU.

2 - The Supply Side

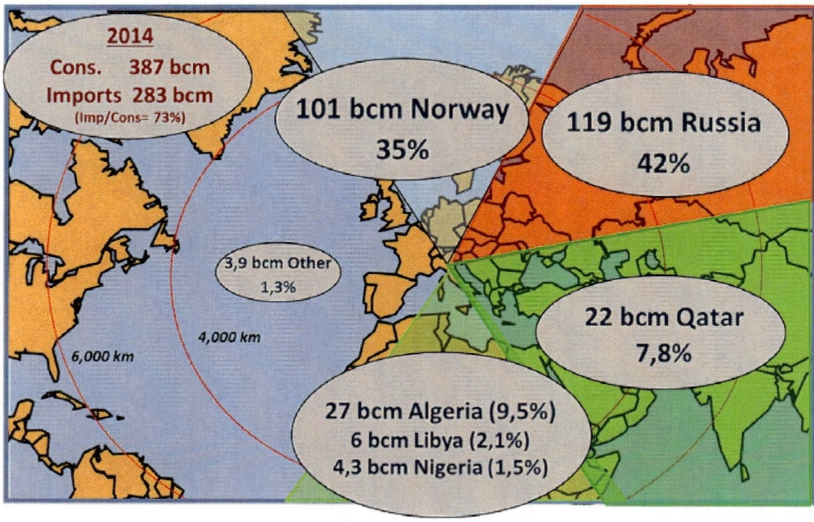

Figure 15. EU gas supply map - 2014. Source: authors' elaboration on BP (2015).

The following sections will focus on this issue, by providing a critical assessment of the current situation and future outlook of key EU gas suppliers (Russia, Norway, Algeria, Libya, LNG) and of perspective suppliers (Eastern Mediterranean, Southern Gas Corridor).

The EU-Russia gas partnership after the 2014 Ukraine crisis

The dawn of the 2014 Ukraine crisis dates back to November 21, 2013, the day on which then-Ukraine's President Viktor Yanukovych rejected the Ukraine-EU Association Agreement and the related Deep and Comprehensive Free Trade Agreement. These two measures of economic and trade incentives were offered by the EU to Ukraine within the framework of the Eastern partnership, an initiative aimed at strengthening cooperation with countries in the former USSR and implicitly containing the influence of Russia in the region.

On the same day, thousands of people gathered to Independence Square in central Kiev to take part in a rally against the choices of Yanukovych and in favor of greater integration with the EU. From that moment on the Euromaidan protests never stopped, finally leading to the deposition of Yanukovych and to the establishment of a pro-European government at the end of February 2014. This move further polarized the Ukraininan society, paving the way for major discontent in its Russian-speaking part, which did not recongize the legitimacy of the regime change. In this context, Russian forces began to gradually take control of the Crimean peninsula. In the meantime, a referendum on the status of Crimea was held on March 16, resulting in a 96% vote in favor of the option to join Russia as a federal subject. The legitimacy of the referendum was immediately rejected by the EU, the US and Canada, while

Russia instantly recognized the result. On March 18 Russia and Crimea finally signed a treaty of accession of the Republic of Crimea and Sevastopol into the Russian Federation, triggering a deeper diplomatic standoff between Russia and the EU. In addition to this, in the Eastern part of Ukraine a pro-Russian independentist movement started to rise, also with the informal support of Russia. This led to an open civil war. These events further deteriorated the EU-Russia relations. This did not only impact the EU's and Russia's foreign policies but also their respective energy policies, with a predominant focus on gas.

The EU took the Ukraine crisis as a further stimulus for its long-lasting gas diversification policy. The new Juncker Commission put energy at the top of its agenda, unleashing the Energy Union initiative, not by case created with a primary focus on security of gas supply. In this framework the new Commission reinvigorated its effort to strengthen ties with current and perspective gas suppliers in the Mediterranean and in the Southern Gas Corridor region and to further develop LNG and internal interconnections.

The EU took the Ukraine crisis as a further stimulus for its long-lasting gas diversification policy.

In this context, Russia remained committed to export its gas to Europe, confirming that the EU-Russia gas partnership should be read as a situation of mutual interdependence rather than unilateral dependence of Europe. In other words, Russia is willing to sell and to continue to sell gas to Europe, as it represents the cornerstone of its export architecture. Russia considers a fundamental prerequiste to ensure the stability of this trade relation to reduce the role of Ukraine as a transit corridor for Russian gas to Europe in order to avoid transit problems as occurred in 2006 and 2009. However, the target announced in 2015 to reduce the transit through Ukraine to zero can also be seen as politically motivated.

Of course, this strategy (underpinning several past and present projects such as Yamal-Europe, Nord Stream, South Stream and Turkish Stream) is not in line with the policy priorities of the EU, which supports the role of Ukraine as a transit country, also in order to guarantee to the Ukrainian state an important source of revenues.

Seeing the negative signals coming from Brussels on the future gas cooperation outlook, Russia also speeded-up its negotiations with China and, after a decade of talks, signed in May 2014 a contract to open-up the so-called 'Eastern route' (a project for the delivery of 38 Bcm/y of Russian gas to China via the Power of Siberia gas pipeline). In November 2014 another framework agreement was signed by Russia and China, this time for the launch of the so-called 'Western route', a project for the delivery of 30 Bcm/y of Russian gas to China via the Altai gas pipeline (Figure 16).

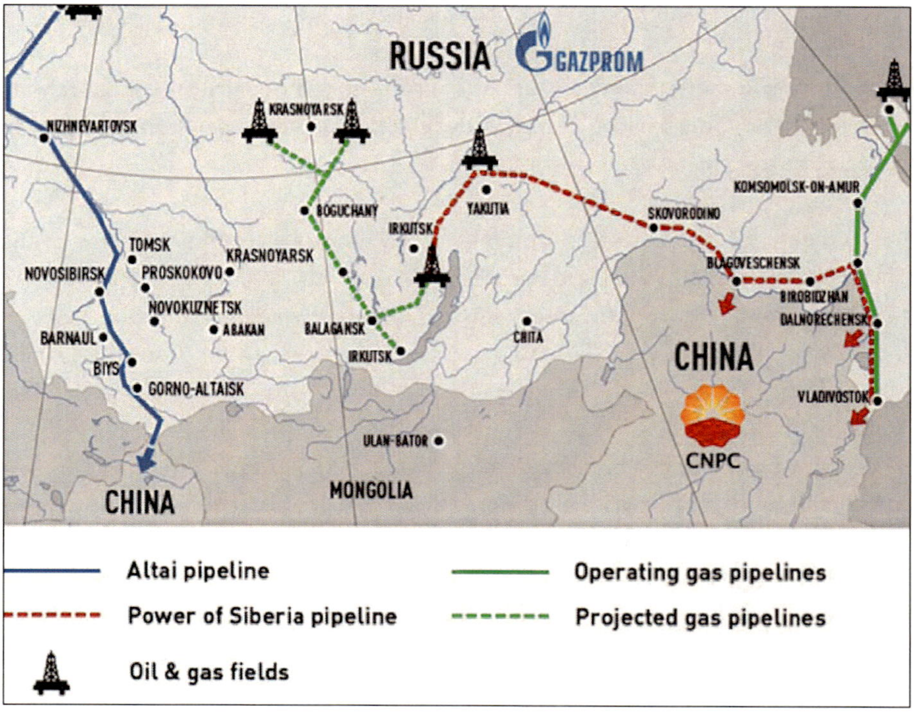

Figure 16. The Russia-China gas pipelines map. Source: Gazprom.

While the Power of Siberia pipeline relies on new gas to be developed in Eastern Siberia, the Altai gas pipeline is supposed to rely on gas coming from Western Siberia (i.e. the very same gas intended for European gas markets).

However, this diversification effort soon proved to be more difficult than previously estimated due to the unprecedented fall in oil prices. In fact, Russia was supposed to deliver gas to the Chinese market on an oil-index basis. With the rapid fall in prices, this framework soon became uneconomic. In addition to this, a secondary element of difficulty emerged to be the present economic slowdown in China.

In addition to this, also the second diversification tool that Russia might have had at its disposal, liquefied natural gas (LNG), was considerably weakened, this time due to international sanctions that, among other things, also target specific technological components needed to develop LNG facilities.

In short, during more than two years of unprecedented political standoffs with the EU over Ukraine, diversification of gas destination markets away from Europe has proved to be a difficult exercise for Russia.

In the meantime, the European Commission adopted a strict interpretation of the Third Energy Package, leading to the failure of the South Stream pipeline project. After years of talks about South Stream, Russian President Vladimir Putin thus declared in Ankara on December 1, 2014 the demise of the project and the launch of a new alternative project to Turkey.[8] After this declaration, Gazprom CEO specified that Russia's plan was to construct a new pipeline under the Black Sea to Turkey with the same capacity of South Stream (63 Bcm/y), to supply 14 Bcm/y to Turkey and the rest to be used for a gas hub on the border with Greece. He also declared that primary aim of the pipeline was to completely eliminate Ukraine from Russia's gas transit to Europe. The pipeline was set to start at the Russkaya pumping station on the Russian coast of the Black Sea, which was supposed to be also the starting point of South Stream. Miller also said that an agreement on the pipeline was previously reached with Turkey and the sides already signed a Memorandum of Understanding (MoU).[9] Turkish Stream, as it would have been successively named, was then already taking shape. After two months of discussions between the Russian and Turkish counterparts on the potential routes of the new pipeline, Gazprom CEO and then-Turkish Minister for Energy and Natural Resources Taner Yildiz presented on February 7, 2015 the latest route of Turkish Stream (Figure 17).

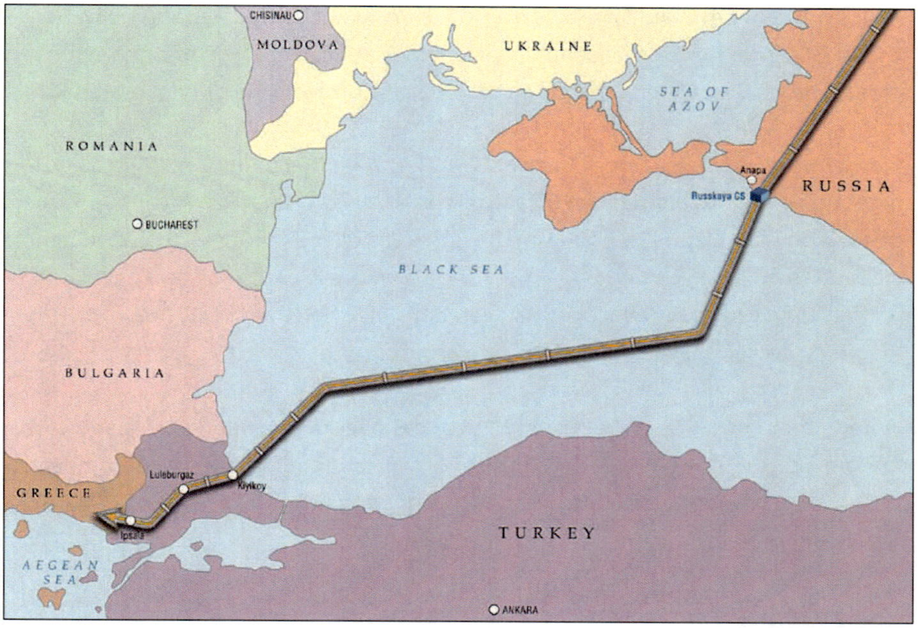

Figure 17. Turkish Stream. Source: Gazprom (official map based on the Russian view of Ukraine's boundaries).

The pipeline would run for 660 km from the Russkaya pumping station on the Russian coast of the Black Sea along the old route of South Stream up to the Bulgarian exclusive economic zone, after which a new 250 km route would dip southwest and run through the Turkish zone to the Turkish coast, near the village of Kiyikoy. According to Gazprom, the gas delivery point for Turkish consumers would be in Luleburgaz, while a connection between Turkey and Greece is planned in Ipsala. After the 910 km in the offshore Black Sea, the pipeline would thus run for additional 180 km on the onshore Turkish territory.[10] Gazprom declared its intention to advance the construction of the pipeline's initial strings (with a capacity of 14 Bcm/y, which correspond to the volume of gas that Turkey currently imports from Russia through Ukraine) by December 2016.[11]

In this plan, it would have been up to European TSOs to construct the infrastructure needed to connect the Turkish Stream delivery point at the Turkish-Greek border with destination markets in Central-western Europe. However, considering the geo-political impasse between the EU and Russia, this perspective did not materialize.

Furthermore, the evolution of the Russia-Turkey relations did not help the development of Turkish Stream neither. In fact, the project was slowed-down due to Turkey's internal political instability in view of the general elections of June 2015. When these elections resulted in a hung parliament and coalition negotiations broke down, Turkish President Erdoğan called for snap elections in November 2015, thus further prolonging the political vacuum in the country.

In addition to this, the unprecedented political standoff between Russia and Turkey followed to the dawning of the Russian aircraft by the Turkish Air Force near the Syria-Turkey border on 24 November 2015 signed the definitive freezing of the Turkish Stream project.

In this overall uncertain situation, Russia came-up in June 2015 with another proposal targeting the European market: the doubling of Nord Stream (Figure 18). Gazprom and its European partners (E.ON, Shell, OMV, BASF and ENGIE) signed a shareholders agreement to construct the 55 Bcm/y Nord Stream II pipeline as an alternative solution to an increasingly-difficult full-scale version of Turkish Stream. With this volume the total capacity of Nord Stream would thus represent 110 Bcm/y (i.e. a capacity almost equal to all present Russian gas export volumes to Europe).

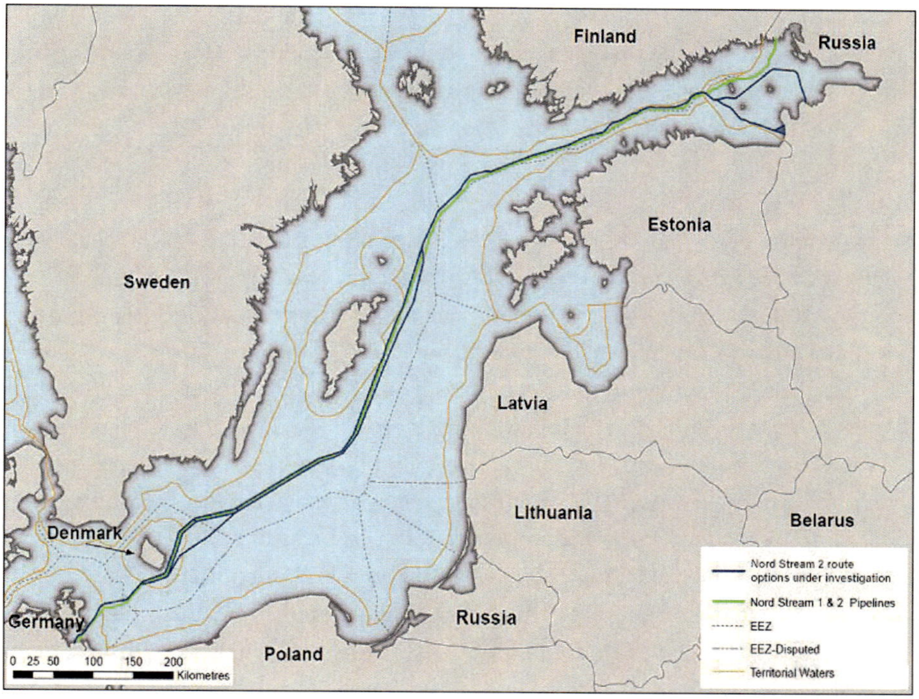

Figure 18. Nord Stream I & II. Source: Nord Stream II.

At the same time Gazprom also conducted a series of gas sales auctions in order to introduce a new pricing mechanism in its key export market: Germany. For some experts, with this move Gazprom appeared to have taken further steps towards the adoption of a new market model in Europe - fundamentally based on spot pricing, while for others the auctions might also have been a tool used by Gazprom to acquire further evidence to support its claims to the EC about the full access of the Opal pipeline capacity, an issue representing a key bottleneck for the full utilization of Nord Stream I, and thus for the feasibility of the Nord Stream II project. In fact, while the auctions showed the interest of buyers to purchase lots at other delivery points, they also showed basically no demand for alternative supplies via Opal. On the basis of this auction, Gazprom could then argue that the European Commission should allow it to use the full pipeline, instead of leaving half of it empty while waiting for potential customers that might never materialize. It thus surprises the decision of the European Commission to limit the utilization of a pipeline to 50 percent for Third Party Access reasons as long as there is not other gas to be shipped through. In any case the problem could also be easily solved from the Gazprom side, by organizing a gas release program on the Nord Stream gas before entering the German market.

Furthermore, always in September 2015, Gazprom finalized key asset swap deals with Germany's BASF and Austria's OMV. Under the deal with BASF, Gazprom took control of jointly operated gas trading and storage businesses, including the biggest gas storage facility in Western Europe. It also received a 50 percent stake in Wintershall's North Sea operations. In exchange, Wintershall received stakes in two fields in Western Siberia, to be jointly developed with Gazprom. Under the deal with OMV, Gazprom has conceded stakes in a field in Western Siberia in exchange for the participating interest in OMV. For many analysts these moves signaled a U-turn in Gazprom's strategy towards Europe as after the demise of South Stream the company claimed to be reluctant to be involved in the European market (i.e. in downstream and midstream activities) due to its complex regulations, and to rather prefer to deliver supplies at the European border - as actually shown by the structure of the Turkish Stream project.

After the 2014 Ukraine crisis the EU-Russia gas relations have basically assisted to two opposite trends.

On the basis of this *excursus* it is well possible to affirm that after the 2014 Ukraine crisis the EU-Russia gas relations have basically assisted to a two, opposite, trends. On the one hand cooperation between Gazprom and European companies continued and even expanded, as demonstrated by Nord Stream II, the German auctions and the swap deals in Germany and Austria. On the other hand the EU-Russia gas partnership has remained frozen at the institutional level, with no signs of rapprochement. This situation not only signals the different approaches being adopted vis-à-vis Russia by the EU institutions and European oil and gas companies, but also the different political stances in the field of the EU institutions and of certain EU Member States. Considering the difficulty of finding a common EU perspective on how gas relations with Russia should develop (due to different Member States' interests in the field), it is possible to expect the EU-Russia gas relations to be carried out with an à-la-carte approach of individual companies (formally or informally supported by the respective Member States) cooperating with Gazprom on single projects (rather than with a more holistic and institutionally-driven approach) as it has always been the case in history.

The outlook of other EU traditional pipeline suppliers: Norway, Algeria, Libya

Norway

Norway has always been a reliable gas supplier to the EU, but some concerns are emerging about its capability to deliver its gas supply in the long-term. The oil output of Norway peaked in 2000. As tax revenues from hydrocarbon extraction represent an important share of Norway's state budget, the declining oil output over the last decade was one of the driving forces behind Norway's impressive gas development. Norway exported in 2014 about 100 Bcm of gas, almost twice the amount of a decade ago. However, it is a matter of fact that Norway has not made a significant gas discovery since the discovery of the Ormen Langen field in 1997. This field, originally assessed at 400 Bcm, has also been successively downgraded to 220 Bcm.

The outlook of other EU traditional pipeline suppliers: Norway, Algeria, Libya

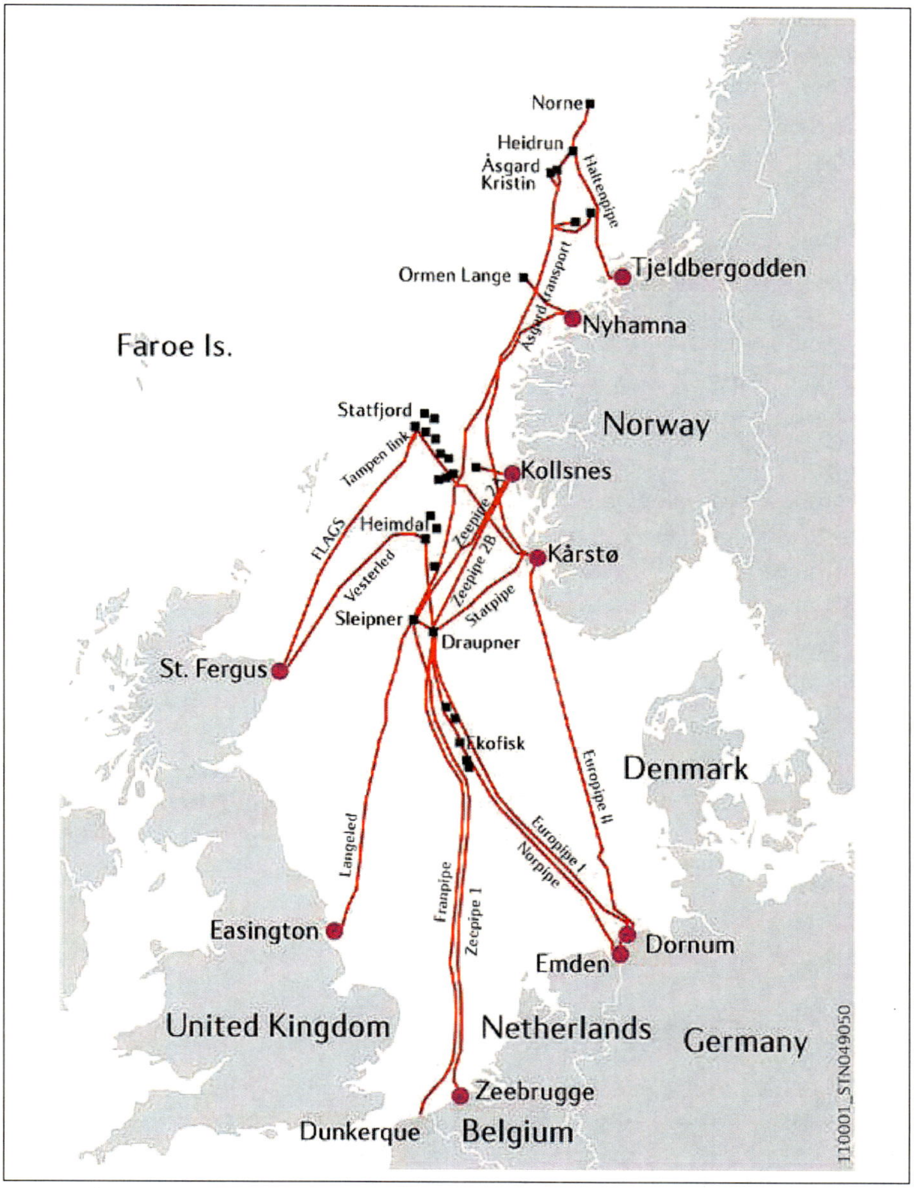

Figure 19. Norway's gas infrastructure. Source: Statoil.

One-third of Norwegian gas production is concentrated in the giant Troll field, which holds over 1 Tcm of gas reserves and has potential for incremental production. Another 20% comes from the previously mentioned Orman Langen field, which can continue producing at current rates during most of this decade. However, no such other giant field is planned to come on stream in the medium term. Fields recently started or planned to start by 2020 have reserves lower than 50 Bcm. This can complicate the development of the next generation of fields unless they are located near the existing transport system, as such a small size does not incentivise development of long-distance pipelines.

In this context, it is impossible to accurately predict how much gas can be produced from the Norwegian Continental Shelf over the next decades. Considerable uncertainty is associated with factors such as geology, reservoir conditions, technology and knowledge development, costs and commodity prices. According to the Norwegian Petroleum Directorate, the country's gas production will peak around 2020 at a level of 105-130 Bcm/y. The successive developments will largely be determined by the new discoveries made in the years to come (Figure 20).

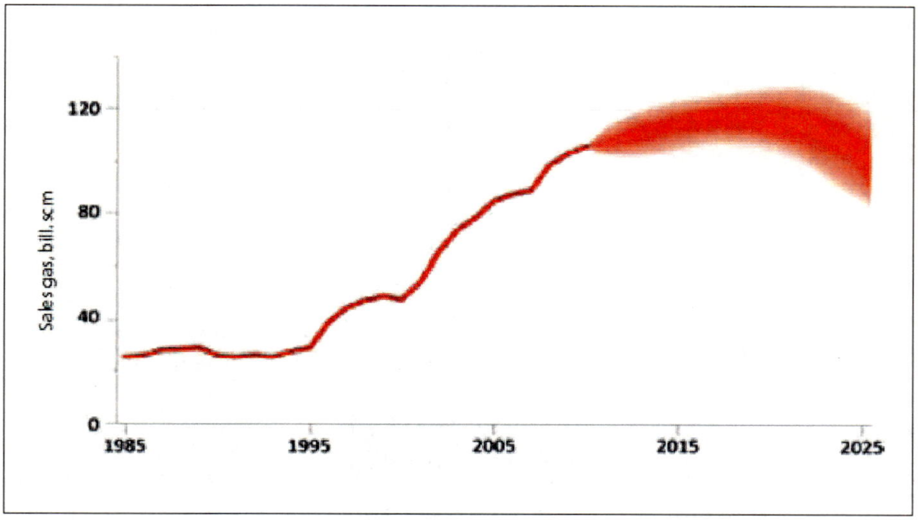

Figure 20. Norwegian gas production outlook. Source: Norwegian Petroleum Directorate.

The key objective of Norway's petroleum policy is to facilitate profitable production of oil and gas in a long-term perspective with a prudent management of the environmental and safety risks associated with this activity. The aim of the government is to combine Norway's role as a major energy producer with the ambition of being a world leader in environmental and climate policy. In this framework, a steady gas production activity will likely be maintained in Norway in order to achieve the goal of long-term management and value creation from the petroleum resources. This activity will most likely focus on both increasing recovery from existing fields and continuing active exploration of opened acreage, in mature and frontier areas. Such developments, involving new solutions on existing fields, new discoveries in mature areas and new discoveries in less mature areas, will likely proceed in parallel in order to facilitate an overall activity level as stable as possible.

Algeria

In terms of gas reserve estimations, the recent years have been very volatile for Algeria. In fact, the Energy Information Administration (EIA) estimated in 2013 the country's technically recoverable shale gas resources at about 20 tcm, the third largest in the world after China and Argentina. These positive developments on the unconventional side have been accompanied by surprisingly negative news on the conventional side, with the country downgrading its estimated conventional gas reserves from 4.5 tcm to 2.7 tcm[12] at the end of 2015.

But the assessment of gas reserves has not been the only volatile element in the country's gas sector. In fact, as illustrated in Figure 21, also production, consumption and export trends have consistently changed over the last years.

After a boom during the 1990s, the country's gas production has basically stagnated since 2000 within a range of 79-88 bcm/y. Meanwhile, the country's gas consumption has progressively grown over the last decades, to reach an all-time-high of 32 bcm in 2013. Consequently, exports substantially declined over the last years, to a level of 43 bcm in 2013.

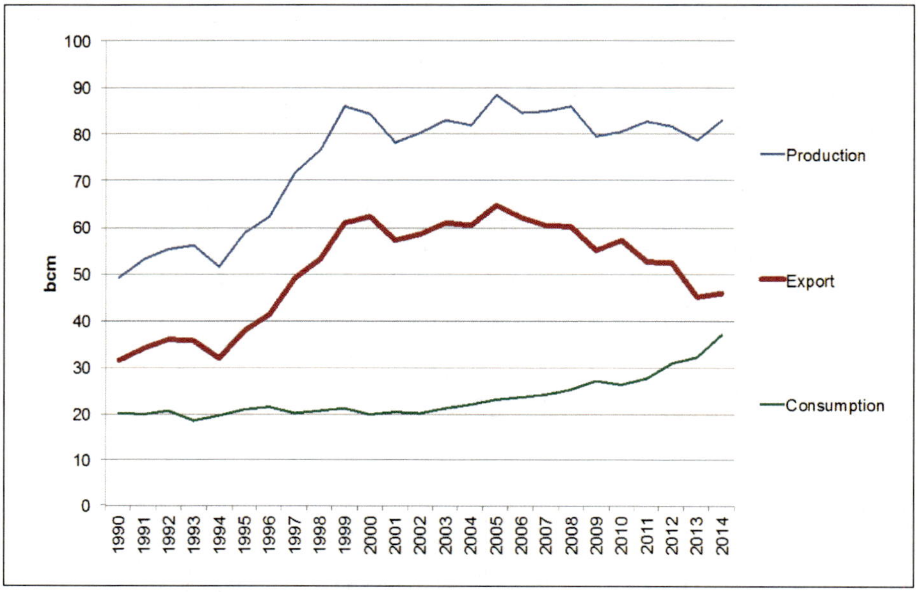

Figure 21. Algeria's natural gas balance (1990-2014). Source: authors' elaboration on BP and IEA.

Under these circumstances, the well-established gas infrastructure (Figure 22) connecting Algeria and Europe has been increasingly underutilized. As indicated in Figure 23, in 2014 Algeria exported 23 bcm of gas via pipeline (out of an export capacity of 54 bcm) and exported 17 bcm of LNG (out of an export capacity of 40 bcm). The magnitude of the 54 bcm of unused capacity is impressive if compared, for example, to the Southern Gas Corridor, the major EU gas supply diversification project, which is expected to deliver 10 bcm/y to the EU by 2020.

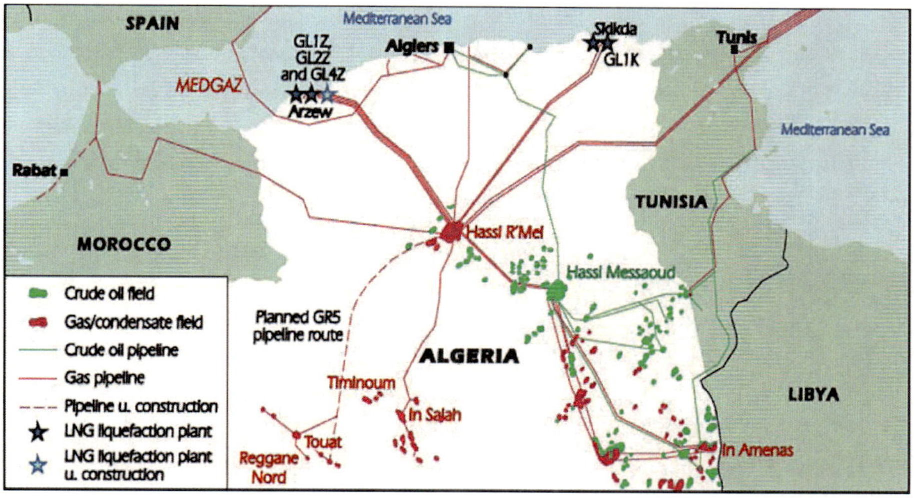

Figure 22. Algeria's oil and gas infrastructure. Source: International Energy Agency.

Bcm	Total export capacity	Export 2014	Excess capacity 2014
Pipeline	54	23	31
LNG	40	17	23
Total	94	40	54

Figure 23. Algeria's underutilized natural gas export infrastructure (2014). Source: authors' elaboration on BP.

The paradox of having a rich gas resource and infrastructure endowments but a poor gas production and export performances is due to a number of institutional and governance bottlenecks.

First of all, the political decision-making process in Algeria is today paralyzed. The uncertain health conditions of President Bouteflika, the long-lasting ruler of the country, are not favoring a timely and efficient policy response to the current challenges also concerning the energy sector.

Secondly, key unresolved issues in the energy sector are the distortion of the market due to energy subsidies, the unattractiveness of the petroleum legal framework, the heaviness of the bureaucratic system, the length of the procedures and the unpredictability in the application of the contractual terms. For all these reasons, the only way Algeria has to enhance its gas production and export performances is to improve the overall governance of its energy sector. This would require a substantial reform of its energy subsidy scheme, and a serious rethinking of its contractual and fiscal terms.

The current low oil price environment represents a key challenge to the macroeconomic sustainability of Algeria, being its economy predominantly based on hydrocarbon revenues. However, this situation might well be seen as an opportunity to justify internally the much-needed reforms in the energy sector, to cut subsidies and to facilitate international investments. Albeit politically difficult in the short term, these actions will be key to sustain the country's energy -and thus overall economic- sector in the longer term.

Libya

Energy speaking, Libya is mainly an oil story but gas also has a role to play in the country's energy sector. Even if smaller than Algeria's, Libya's gas reserves (1.5 tcm) indeed exceed the ones of Azerbaijan (1.2 tcm) - the country leading the development of the already mentioned Southern Gas Corridor.

Libyan gas is piped from the Wafa concession and the offshore Bahr es Salam fields to Mellitah, where it is treated for export. Libya has one LNG terminal (operative since 1971, albeit never fully utilized) located in Marsa El Brega and one international pipeline, Greenstream, that runs from Mellitah to Gela (Sicily) and is operative since 2004.

Because of its small population (about 6 million people, the lowest in North Africa), Libya's domestic gas consumption remains low. However, this might grow in the future particularly due to a greater role of gas in the power generation sector and an eventual role in industrial plants, which would however depend on the expansion of Libya's gas distribution network.

Notwithstanding its considerable reserves, Libya's gas production declined from 17 bcm in 2010 to 12 bcm in 2014 and, consequently, exports to Italy dropped from 10 bcm in 2010 to 6 bcm in 2014.

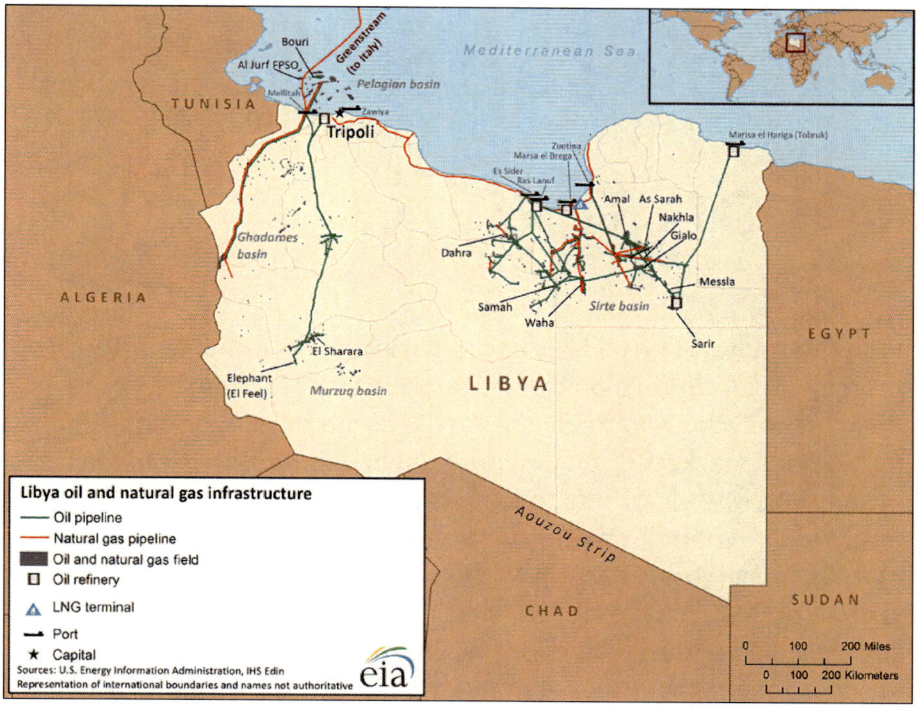

Figure 24. Libya's oil and gas infrastructure. Source: Energy Information Administration.

It is almost impossible to foreseen the potential future development of Libya's gas sector, as this will mainly depend on the evolution of the country's geopolitical situation, which today appears to be extremely volatile and unpredictable.

The prospects for global LNG markets and their repercussions on the EU

Liquefied natural gas (LNG) has represented over the last decade the key driver underpinning the progressive globalisation of international gas markets. In fact, two of the three world's key natural gas markets (Europe and Asia) have become more and more interconnected due to inter-regional LNG trade. This situation might well expand in the future also to the third key natural gas market, North America, due to the entrance of US LNG into the global market. LNG trade, which is projected to continue to grow strongly over the next decades, is also increasing the price links between the three regional markets through the potential for arbitrage. This section sheds light on the key developments of this important market.

Global LNG trade has constantly grown over the last decades. As illustrated in Figure 25, the volume of LNG trade expanded from less than 50 million tons per annum (MTPA) in 1990 to more than 200 MTPA in 2014.

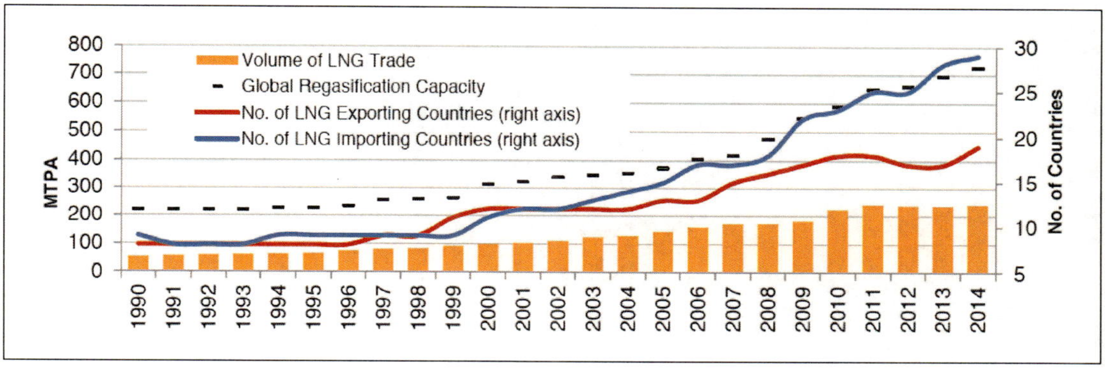

Figure 25. LNG trade volumes (1990-2014). Source: IGU.

Both the number of LNG exporting and importing countries have grown significantly, from about 7 in 1990 to about 20 and 30 respectively in 2014. In 2014 Qatar was the key LNG exporter of the world (covering one-third of global LNG supply), followed by Malaysia, Australia, Nigeria, Indonesia, Trinidad, Algeria, Russia and other minor suppliers. The Middle East thus represents the leading LNG exporting region in the world. In the same year Japan and South Korea imported more than half of global LNG (only Japan imported more than 30 percent), followed by China, India, Taiwan and several other minor importers. Asia and Asia Pacific markets thus represent the most important LNG importing region at global level, with a combined demand of 75 percent in 2014. However, this figure is rapidly evolving, with the Chinese and the Indian markets expected to grow strongly over the next years.

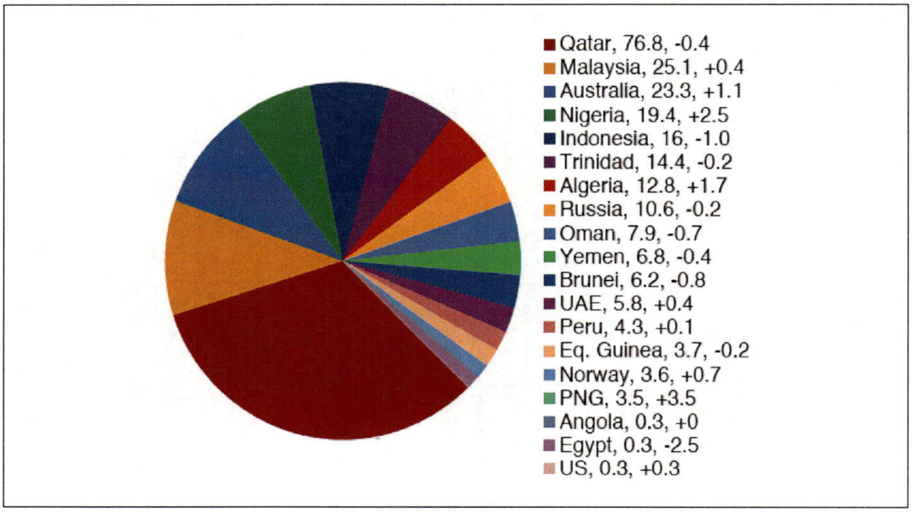

Figure 26. 2014 LNG Exports by Country & Incremental Change Relative to 2013 (MTPA). Source: IGU.

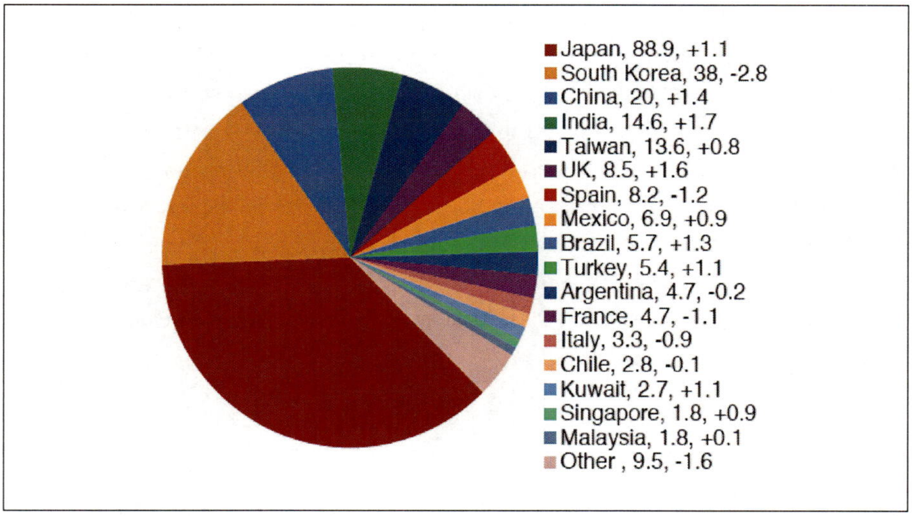

Figure 27. 2014 LNG Imports by Country & Incremental Change Relative to 2013 (MTPA). Source: IGU.

In perspective, the LNG share of inter-regional trade is expected to further rise over the next decades. The IEA estimates that this share will grow from the current level of about 40 percent to 50 percent in 204013. As Figure 28 illustrates, LNG exports are set to rise mainly in Australia, Africa, North America and Russia.

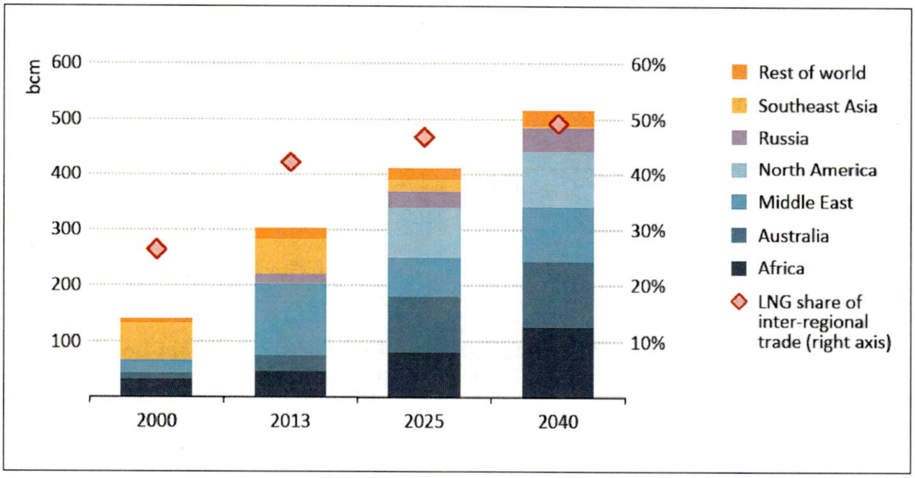

Figure 28. LNG exports by region in the IEA New Policy Scenario. Source: IEA (2015).

The previous figure also indicates a major expansion of LNG exports in the period up to 2025. This reflects the major capacity addition that characterizes the period 2015-2020. In fact, as illustrated in Figure 29, capacity additions tend to come in waves that come in intervals of about five years or more.

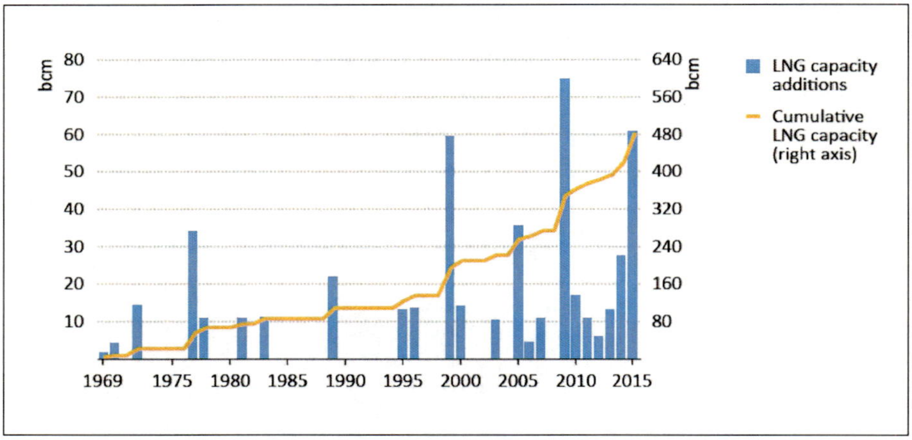

Figure 29. Global LNG liquefaction capacity additions. Source: IEA (2015).

These cycles are driven by gas discoveries, cycles in gas markets and expectations of future demand growth. The year 2015 already signed the beginning of the new cycle with a capacity addition of 60 bcm. This cycle will gather further pace with major projects coming online by 2020 in Australia and the United States. Australia has seven new LNG projects coming online or under construction, that will expand its exports from 26 bcm in 2013 to 90 bcm per year in 2020. At the same time, the United States - with Sabine Pass and other four projects under construction - are also set to expand their exports to 90 bcm per year in 2020.[14]

This expanding cycle will have a strong impact on the LNG market over the next years, also in terms of pricing. In fact, gas importers are expected to benefit from this situation as growing supply will put a downward pressure on prices all over the world. This trend will be further emphasized by the fact that even if LNG continues to be mainly based on long-term trade, in relative terms spot and short-term trade has substantially increased over the last decades, rising from zero percent in 1995 to about 27 percent in 2014.

China and India will certainly absorb much of the new available supply but considering that Japan will progressively reopen its nuclear reactors is difficult to expect Asia to take all the new available additional volumes. For this reason, Europe has certainly an opportunity to have access to low-priced LNG in the period up to 2020. However, this favourable situation for LNG importers might well revers in the 2020s, with a new cycle of tighter markets resulting from delayed investment in new LNG projects due to low prices in the period 2015-2020. In fact, many greenfield LNG projects (thus expected to come online after 2020) are already been reconsidered all over the world from Africa to Australia, to North America. For instance, the prospects of a new wave of post-2020 Australian projects is being reconsidered after announcements of final investment decision postponements or even project cancellations from different international companies. The same phenomenon is also already appearing in Canada and in Russia.

To focus on the prospects for Europe in the period up to 2020, it is possible to expect that dropping LNG prices will strongly affect the overall structure of European gas markets. In fact, the availability of low-cost LNG will put pressure on gas producers such as Russia, Algeria and Norway, which will have to decide on whether to defend its existing pricing formulae or defend its market share by competing with LNG suppliers.

This is particularly true if considering that about 150 bcm of gas import contracts to the EU are set to expire over the next ten years.[15] However, it should be noted that among the three key pipeline gas suppliers to Europe, Russia enjoys the most resilient contracts for the next decade (Figure 30).

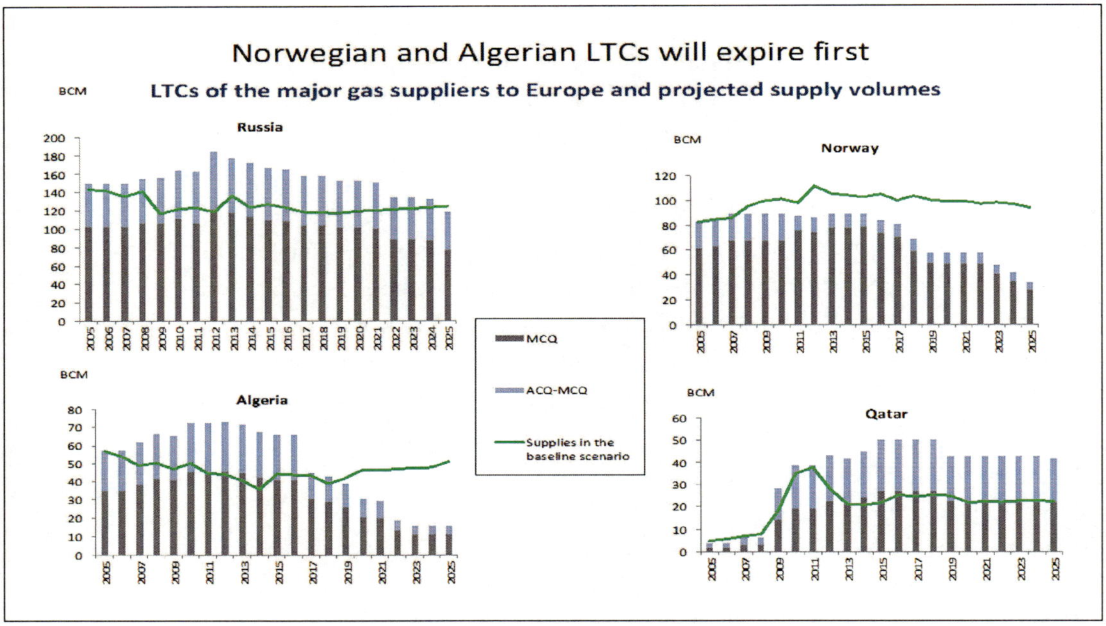

Figure 30. Long term contracts of the major gas suppliers to Europe. Source: ERIRAS (2016). [MCQ: minimum contracted quantities; ACQ: average contracted quantities].

In this context, Russia will still have 80 bcm of minimum contracted quantity by 2025 (down from 100 bcm today). On this basis Russia is contractually well protected against a massive wave of LNG expected to materialize in the second half of the present decade. This is not the case of Algeria and Norway, which are thus much more exposed.

Having said this, Russia will most likely be committed to export to Europe much more than the minimum contracted quantities and for this reason Gazprom has already announced that it will fight for market share in Europe. As a matter of fact, already over the last years Russia has been selling its volumes above the minimum contracted quantities mainly at spot basis. Therefore, it is well possible to expect a future price war in Europe with LNG competing with Russian gas at spot basis. The case for such a development is also entailed in the fact that in Europe over the last ten years spot pricing increased from 15 to 60 percent on average (Figure 31). This ratio represents already 90 percent in North-western Europe, a region that represents 50 percent of European gas markets[16] and where a competition between LNG and Russia gas is already in place (Figure 32).

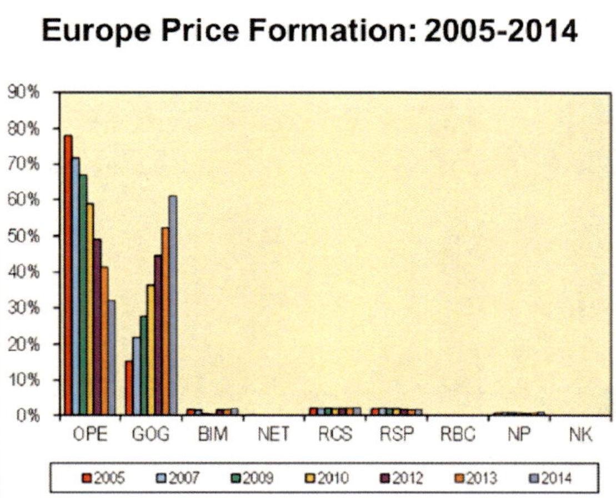

Europe Gas Supply by destination and pricing: Q4-2014

Region and approx. % of total European demand	OPE	GOG	RCS	RSP	BIM	NP
North West Europe 50%	12	88				
Central Europe 15%	32	53		15		
Med. Europe 30%	64	30				6
South East Europe 5%	38	4	52	4		2
			3	2		2
Europe Total	32	61	7			

OPE: Oil Price Escalation GOG: Gas-on-Gas Competition RCS: Regulated Price (Cost of Service) RSP: Regulated Price (Social and Political) BIM: Bilateral Monopoly NP: No Price North West Europe: Belgium, Denmark, France, Germany, Ireland, Netherlands, UK. Central Europe: Austria, Czech Rep, Hungary, Poland, Slovakia, Switzerland. Mediterranean Europe: Portugal, Spain, Italy, Greece, Turkey. South East Europe: Bosnia, Bulgaria, Croatia, Macedonia, Romania, Serbia, Slovenia.

Figure 31. Evolution of European gas price formation. (2005-2014). Source: Heather (2015).

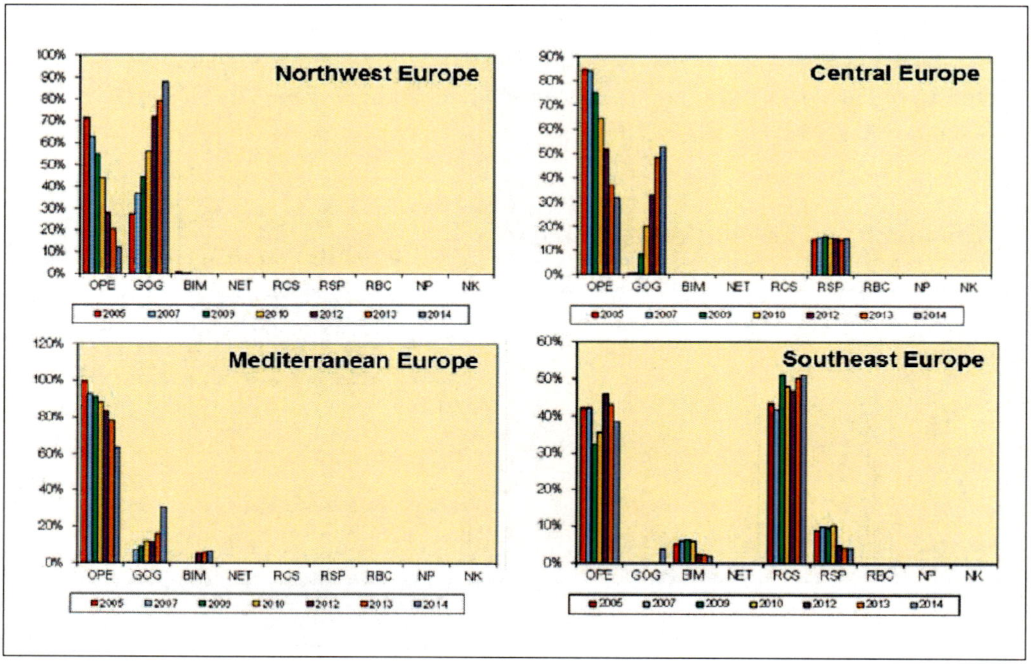

Figure 32. Evolution of regional European gas price formation. (2005-2014). Source: Heather (2015).

To conclude with our analysis of LNG markets and their impact on the EU, it should be outlined that Europe not only has a well-established LNG infrastructure (Figure 33), but this is also currently strongly under-utilized at the impressive level of 68 percent (or 124 bcm, a level corresponding to Russia's gas exports to the EU), thus providing a huge margin for additional LNG imports (Figure 34).

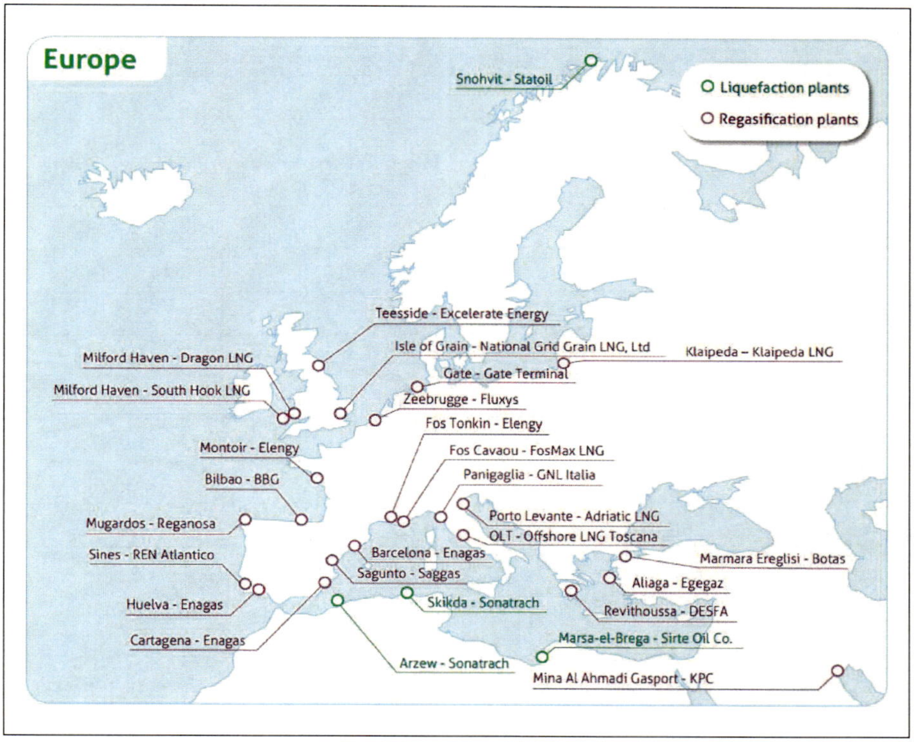

Figure 33. LNG infrastructure in Europe. Source: GIIGNL.

Country	Capacity	Imports in 2014 (Net of re-exports)	Utilization rate
Spain	60.2	17.6	29.2%
United Kingdom	50.7	18.5	36.5%
France	25.3	10.1	39.9%
Italy	15.3	7.2	47.1%
Netherlands	12	0.9	7.5%
Belgium	9	2.1	23.3%
Portugal	5.5	2.1	38.2%
Greece	5.2	0.8	15.4%
Lithuania	4	n.a.	n.a.
Sweden	0.3	n.a.	n.a.
TOTAL	183.5	59.3	32.3%

Figure 34. Utilization rate of the EU's LNG infrastructure (2014). Source: authors' elaboration on GIE.

The large under-utilization of the EU's LNG import infrastructure does not, however, imply that all these volumes could concretely be brought where needed in the EU. In fact, interconnections and reverse flows systems are still missing among various EU member states, creating a physical limit to the exploitation of the continent's LNG potential. For this reason, the creation of a truly interconnected and flexible EU gas market remains a key policy priority for the European institutions - as the final part of this book will illustrate.

New supply potential: the Eastern Mediterranean and the Southern Gas Corridor

Looking into the future, European gas markets might also benefit from two new opportunities emerging in the region: the potential creation of a new Eastern Mediterranean gas hub in the aftermath of the recent discovery of the massive Zohr field in offshore Egypt and the materialization of the long-awaited Southern Gas Corridor.

Towards an Eastern Mediterranean gas hub?

Over the last years the Eastern Mediterranean has represented a bestseller story of international gas markets. With the 2009/2010 discoveries of the Tamar and Leviathan fields in offshore Israel and the 2011 discovery of the Aphrodite field in offshore Cyrpus, an unprecedented momentum emerged about the potential rise of the area as a new hotspot in the regional gas markets (Figure 35).

2 – The Supply Side

Gas field	Country	Year of discovery	Resources
Tamar	Israel	2009	280 bcm Gross mean resources
Leviathan	Israel	2010	620 bcm Gross mean resources
Aphrodite	Cyrpus	2011	140 bcm Gross mean resources
Zohr	Egypt	2015	850 bcm Potential of lean gas in place

Figure 35. Key recent gas discoveries in the Eastern Mediterranean. Source: author's elaboration on Eni (2015) and Noble Energy (2015).

On the commercial side, a wide range of export options started to be proposed and discussed, either in form of pipeline (from the one to Turkey to the one to Greece) and of liquefied natural gas – LNG – (from the Vasilikos project in Cyprus to the option of using the idle LNG plants in Egypt, let alone other projects such as floating LNG or onshore LNG plants in Israel -from the Mediterranean to the Gulf of Aqaba).

On the geopolitical side, a full-fledged debate emerged about the potential role of the new gas discoveries not only in creating regional energy cooperation but also in paving the way for a new era of economic and political stability in the region. However, this initial momentum progressively slowed-down vis-à-vis the numerous commercial, political and technical challenges facing the development prospects of the new gas discoveries.

For instance, in Israel a long-lasting internal political debate on the management of the gas resources created a climate of uncertainty that contributed to the delay of key investment decisions. Meanwhile, in Cyprus – where the gas discovery was welcomed as a godsend potentially able to relief the country from its financial troubles- the initial enthusiasm was cooled-down by successive downsizings of the initially expected resources.

In short, albeit for different reasons, neither Israel nor Cyprus have been able to turn (individually or jointly) their gas potential into reality. In this framework, the expectations of seeing the Eastern Mediterranean becoming a gas-exporting region have progressively weakened, unleashing a general sense of skepticism on this regard.

All of a sudden, these expectations have recently been revived by the discovery of the large Zohr gas field in offshore Egypt. Considering its size, this discovery - the largest ever made in the Mediterranean Sea - might potentially represent a game-changer for the regional gas outlook. However, geopolitics is the factor that will ultimately define whether this new development would remain confined to Egypt or would systemically impact the overall Eastern Mediterranean region. Let's see why.

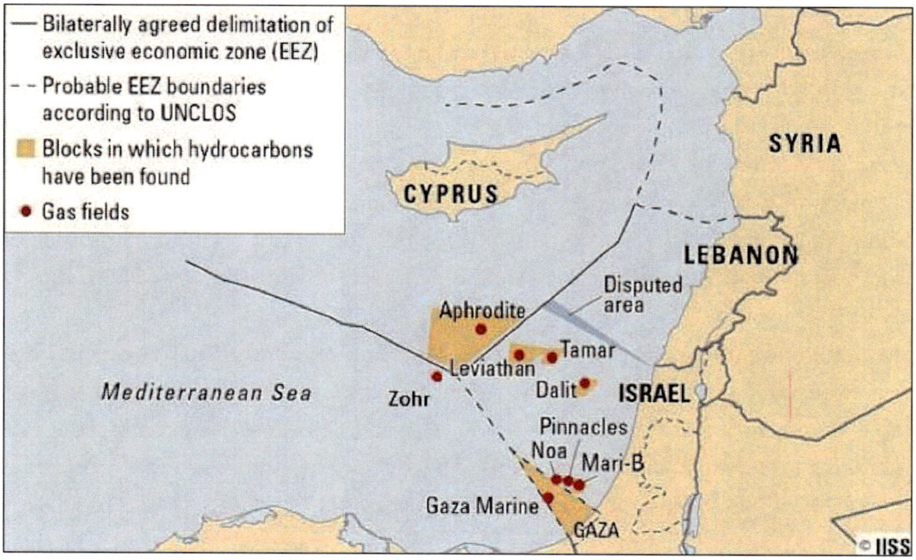

Figure 36. The East Mediterranean gas landscape. Source: IISS (2015).

If there is a certainty about Zohr, it is that its development will primarily serve the Egyptian domestic market. In fact, due to a rapid decline in production the country has increasingly struggled over the last years to meet its own domestic demand. As a result of this, in 2015 Egypt even started to import gas through two floating storage and regasification units (FSRU) leased for five years. In this framework, Egypt's LNG exports dropped from a level of about 15 Bcm/year in 2005 to almost zero in 2014, leaving the country's two LNG plants completely idle. With a potential 20 year-plateau production level of 20-30 Bcm/year Zohr thus represents a major source of relief for Egypt's constrained gas market, as its contribution will be key to make the country's status as gas importer short-lived.

Moreover, Zohr might well be the first of a new string of surprises from the Egyptian offshore. In fact, this discovery is already spurring international oil companies (IOCs) to make new investments in the area. In this context it is well possible to expect Egypt to regain its role of LNG exporter in the post-2020 horizon, as Zohr and other potential offshore fields will approach their plateau production level.

However, the impact of Zohr could well go beyond Egypt's boundaries, particularly if taking into consideration two aspects: geographic proximity and infrastructure.

Zohr only distances 90 km from Aphrodite, which in turn distances only 7 km from Leviathan. This proximity would allow a coordinated development of the fields and thus the creation of the economies of scale needed to put in place a competitive regional gas export monetization scheme.

As mentioned above, Egypt has already in place a 19 Bcm/year LNG export infrastructure, which is currently idle. After having satisfied the domestic market, available volumes from Zohr and other domestic fields might well be exported through this infrastructure. However, part of this capacity might also be used to export Israeli and Cypriot gas. Furthermore, considering that both LNG plants at Idku and Damietta can be expanded with the addition of new trains, if necessary the current capacity might also increase to accommodate further gas volumes.

The combination of these two elements might represent the only way for Israeli and Cypriot gas to reach international markets. In fact, also on the basis of the previously mentioned disappointing past developments, it is increasingly unlikely that the two countries will be able to put in place a commercially viable export option without cooperating with other players in the region for the exploitation of economies of scale. In this framework, Egypt seems to hold the keys of the Eastern Mediterranean gas future. It might decide to proceed alone, by exporting the gas volumes that will progressively become available on top of the domestic demand, or it might decide to proceed together with Israel and Cyprus, by creating a new Eastern Mediterranean gas hub based on its existing exporting infrastructure.

Commercially speaking, this second option looks preferable, as it would represent a win-win situation for all players involved:

1. It would be positive for Egypt, that might considerably enhance its geoeconomic role in the region, alongside its fiscal revenues related to such a transit scheme;

2. It would be positive for Israel and Cyprus, that otherwise would not be able to fully exploit their gas resources, with all the related macroeconomic damages;

3. It would be positive for Europe, which might see the materialization of an unexpected new LNG corridor by a time, the post-2020 horizon, on which its gas import requirements will grow even if demand will continue to stagnate due to rapidly decreasing domestic production and progressively expiring long-term contracts with Norway and Russia.

Albeit commercially soundly, the realization of a new Eastern Mediterranean gas hub will ultimately mainly depend on geopolitical factors. In particular, this will depend on the political willingness of Egypt and Israel to cooperate in such a highly strategic sector. This possibility will be a function of both foreign policy considerations and domestic politics, where the respective public opinions will most likely raise political questions about the opportunity of creating such economic and geopolitical ties in the framework of a volatile geopolitical landscape.

From its side, the EU should support a regional cooperation scheme aimed at developing an Eastern Mediterranean gas hub for both energy policy and foreign policy considerations. In terms of energy policy, this initiative could provide much-needed substance to the long-lasting EU gas supply diversification strategy. In terms of foreign policy, this initiative could represent an important element of international collaboration in an area of the neighborhood that otherwise currently presents -and will most likely continue to present- very little margins of cooperation.

The Southern Gas Corridor: towards the end of the odyssey?

Over the last two decades the Southern Gas Corridor has represented a key topic of any discussion concerning the EU gas security of supply. Since the late 1990s endless speculations have been formulated about the possibility of channelling gas volumes from Azerbaijan, Turkmenistan, Iraq and Iran to Europe via Turkey. However, notwithstanding the political support of the EU, Turkey and even the United States, the initiative never concretely advanced. Launched in 2002, Nabucco – the flagship pipeline project of the Southern Gas Corridor – progressively encountered a number of commercial and financial barriers that prevented its factual realization. This stagnant situation was moved only in 2011, when Azerbaijan (clearly the natural gas producing country most interested on the development of the Southern Gas Corridor[17]) completely reshaped the regional gas game by rapidly conceptualizing its own infrastructure project to evacuate future gas flows from its Shah Deniz Phase II field to Turkey and Europe: the Trans-Anatolian Pipeline (TANAP).

Azerbaijan completely reshaped the regional gas game by rapidly conceptualizing its own infrastructure project.

New supply potential: the Eastern Mediterranean and the Southern Gas Corridor

Figure 37. The Southern Gas Corridor Pipeline Projects. Source: Platts (2015).

TANAP, a projected 2,000 km-long natural gas pipeline with a capacity of 16 bcm/year, has been designed to supply 6 bcm/year to Turkey by 2018 and 10 bcm/year to Europe by 2019. On the contrary of the initial Nabucco project, TANAP was not born as a multilateral project but rather as a bilateral project between Azerbaijan and Turkey. Of course this bilateral relation was not symmetric, but rather unbalanced in favour of Azerbaijan. In fact, the State Oil Company of Azerbaijan (SOCAR) was initially set to hold an 80 percent stake in the project, leaving only the remaining 20 percent to the Turkish partners (15 percent to BOTAŞ and 5 percent to TPAO). This figure has changed over time, to a more balanced structure entailing a share of 58 percent for SOCAR, 30 percent for BOTAŞ and 12 percent for BP. Notwithstanding this realignment of shares, SOCAR is set to continue to retain a controlling share of TANAP and operatorship of the line in the future. In fact, TANAP is crucially important for the Azeri state owned company, as it will have a key role in the delivery of natural gas from its Shah Deniz field further down the supply chain to Europe.

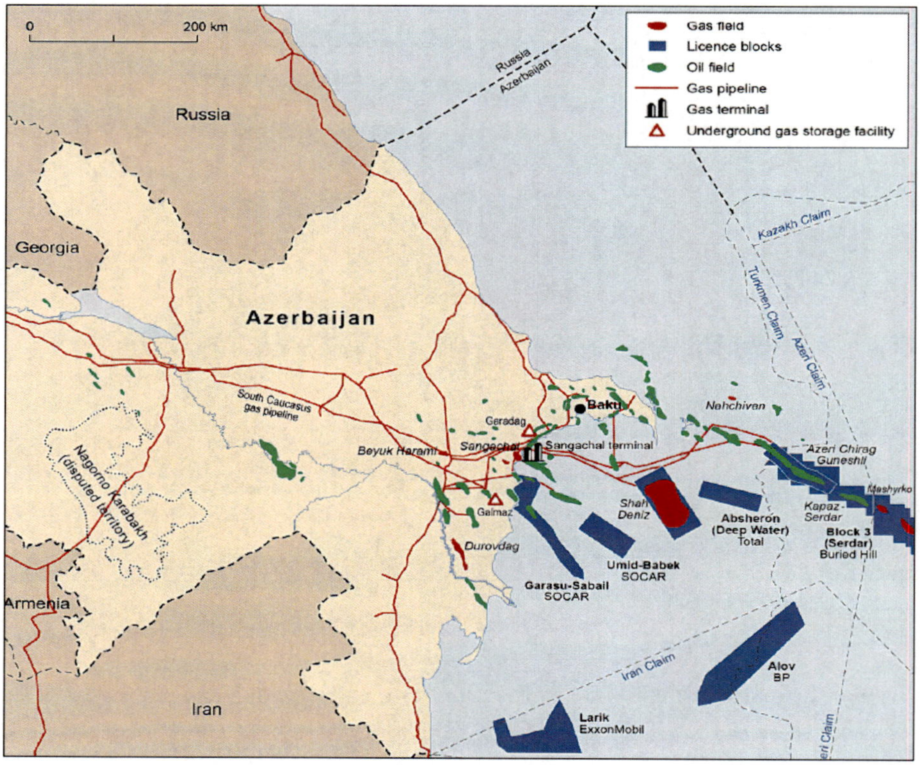

Figure 38. Azerbaijan gas infrastructure. Source: Oxford Institute for Energy Studies (2012).

The entrance of TANAP into the Southern Gas Corridor race in 2011 gave the "coup de grace" to the already moribund Nabucco project. For this reason the Nabucco consortium tried to reinvent itself in 2012, by proposing a new - and smaller - version of the project: Nabucco West.[18] This pipeline was designed to carry the TANAP 10 bcm/year destined to Europe from the Turkish-European border to Austria via Bulgaria, Romania and Hungary. This project - again supported by the EU[19] - ultimately failed like its predecessor, as the Shah Deniz consortium selected in June 2013 the Trans Adriatic Pipeline (TAP) to provide the missing link between TANAP and the European market.[20] TAP, a projected 800 km-long natural gas pipeline with an initial capacity of 10 bcm/year, will thus carry the TANAP natural gas destined to

Europe from the Turkish-Greek border to Italy through Albania and the Adriatic Sea by 2019.[21]

In a nutshell, the 10 bcm/year by 2019 of Azerbaijan are the only tangible input that this initiative will provide to European gas markets in the foreseeable future. In fact, as will be hereafter described, none of the other potential suppliers in the region are likely to join Azerbaijan in this initiative anytime soon.

Turkmenistan

Turkmenistan has established a special natural gas relationship with China, and this trend is likely to consolidate further in the future.

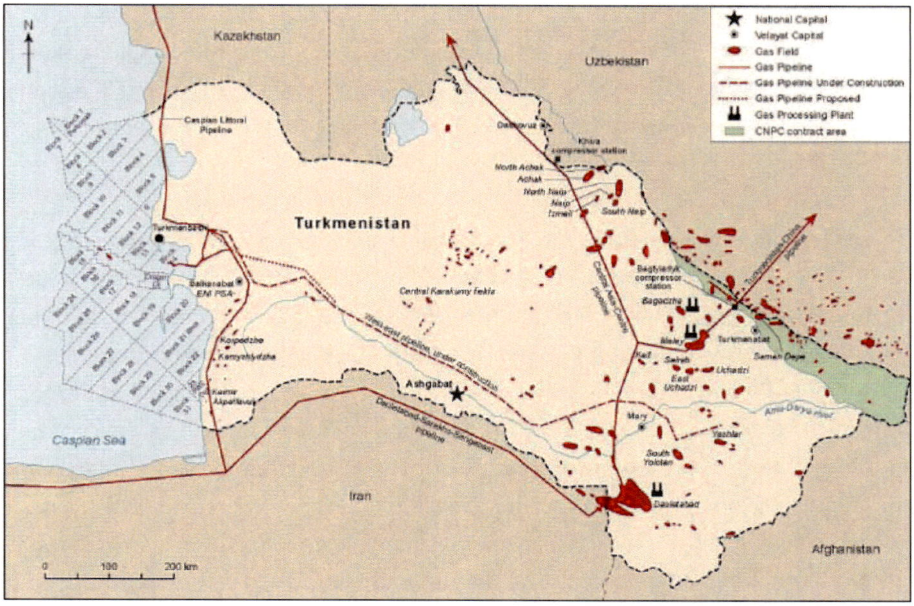

Figure 39. Turkmenistan gas infrastructure. Source: Oxford Institute for Energy Studies (2012).

However, given its world-class gas reserves, the country could well be able to supply natural gas to Turkey and to the EU -in addition to the major volumes targeting the

Chinese market - but a major barrier will likely make such a development unfeasible: the infrastructural problem related to the divergences existing between Russia, Iran, and Turkmenistan on the legal status of the Caspian Sea, and therefore on the construction of the Trans-Caspian Pipeline.

In order to try to bypass this problem, in 2010 Eni proposed to Azerbaijan and Turkmenistan a compressed natural gas (CNG) project that would permit the transport and transit of considerable volumes of Turkmen gas across the Caspian Sea to the coast of Azerbaijan, from where it would be transported through an overland pipeline to other destinations. At the time, this project was halted by Azerbaijan, as it did not want Turkmen gas to compete with its resources being developed. Such a project could be revived in the future if Azerbaijan would temporarily need additional volumes to fill the TANAP pipeline, while waiting for additional production in Shah Deniz. However, this solution will likely be very costly and very limited in both time and volumes. For this reason, the aspiration of the EU to bring major volumes of Turkmen natural gas into the Southern Gas Corridor via the Caspian Sea would probably need to be revised, at least until the dispute over the legal status of the sea will finally be resolved.[22]

The only option to overcome the traditional difficulties concerning the prospects of Turkmen gas exports to Turkey and the EU might be one of using Iran as a transit country. In fact, with the lift of international sanctions and the comeback of Iran into global energy markets, international energy companies might consider the opportunity of linking Turkmenistan and Turkey with a land pipeline passing through Iran. Such an option might have some interesting spillovers for Iran as well, not only in terms of transit fees but also in terms of overall gas strategy. In fact, being Iran not interested in supplying gas to Europe via pipeline but rather via LNG (as it will soon be illustrated), additional gas volumes coming from Turkmenistan could supply Northern areas of the country, freeing up more 'Iranian' gas (being produced in the South) to be exported via LNG at South Pars or via the perspective Iran-Pakistan(-India) pipeline.

Iraq

The Kurdistan Region of Iraq (KRI) has emerged over the last few years as a potential new gas supplier. With an estimated range of 3-6 tcm of natural gas resources, the KRI might be able to both satisfy its domestic natural gas demand and to export volumes to Turkey and Europe.

Turkey plays an important role in this area, geopolitically and commercially. Turkey and the Kurdistan Regional Government in Erbil signed a natural-gas sales agreement in 2013 for the export of 4 bcm/y by 2017, 10 bcm/y by 2020 and 20 bcm/y thereafter.

Building on this agreement, the Anglo-Turkish company Genel Energy plc reached in November 2014 an agreement with the Kurdistan Regional Government for the development of two natural gas fields, Miran and Bina Bawi, which Genel Energy expects to deliver gross mean sales of about 240 bcm of gas.

Considering the potential resource endowment of the region, natural gas exports from the KRI to Europe via Turkey might also well materialise in the medium term, after the KRI reaches natural gas self-sufficiency and after the Kurdistan Regional Government fulfils its obligations to Turkey. However, such a development will depend on internal regulatory stability and regional geopolitics.

A major barrier to the development of the KRI's energy resources has been the tensions between Erbil and Baghdad over the distribution of oil revenues. In December 2014 the two parties finalised a deal to ease these tensions, which might ultimately pave the way for a new Iraqi federal hydrocarbon law, which would enhance foreign investors' confidence in the country.

Of course, the unpredictable evolution of regional geopolitics and the security situation in Iraq will ultimately determine the pace of this development.

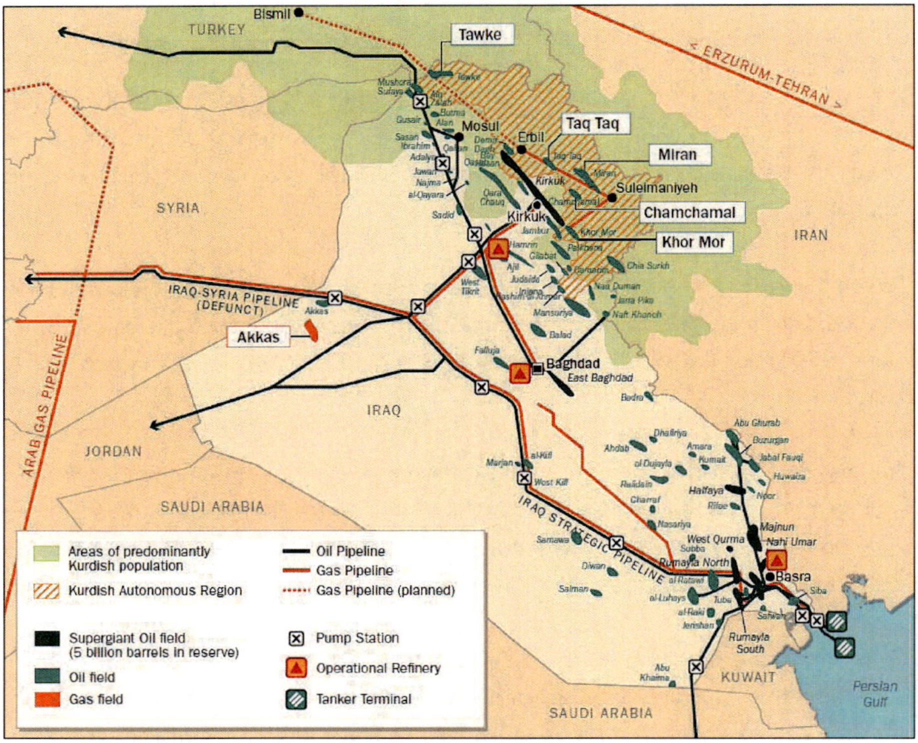

Figure 40. Iraq gas infrastructure. Source: Platts (2014).

Iran

With its 34 tcm of gas reserves, the largest in the world according to BP, Iran is generally considered the main prize for the international gas trade. Notwithstanding this rich natural endowment, the country has not yet translated potential into reality and, paradoxically, even continues to have problems in meeting its own domestic natural gas demand.

Over the last years two have been the key reasons for the under-exploitation of Iran's gas resources: the international sanctions regime and the country's legal framework in relation to petroleum.

Now that international sanctions have been lifted, the reform of the country's legal framework stands as the key barrier in this field. At the end of November 2015, President Hassan Rouhani's government proposed extensive changes to the regulation of oil production, seeking to make investment in Iran more attractive to international companies. However, this proposed reform has been criticized by the opposition, which accuse Rouhani of going against the constitution, which strictly prohibits foreign ownership of the country's natural resources. In fact, the Iranian constitution, adopted after the Islamic Revolution of 1979, states that "public wealth and property, such as uncultivated or abandoned land, mineral deposits, seas, [...], shall be at the disposal of the Islamic government for it to utilize in accordance with the public interest." On this basis, the constitution also "absolutely" forbids "the granting of concessions to foreigners for the formation of companies or institutions dealing with commerce, industry, agriculture, services or mineral extraction [...]."

From 1979 to 1998 Iran did not sign any petroleum agreements with international oil companies. The government only started to pay attention to the development of the country's oil and gas industry under President Mohammad Khatami, who was in office from 1997 to 2005. In order to attract the necessary foreign capital and expertise to develop the petroleum industry, the government introduced a new legal framework, the buy-back service contract (BBSC). Under this scheme, international oil companies can agree to carry out the necessary exploration activities to develop an oil or gas field, but must hand the field over to the National Iranian Oil Company (NIOC) once production starts. The scheme overcomes the constitutional constraints on oil production. However, the programme is unattractive for foreign oil companies, which have to make large investments, and then hand the asset back to the Iranian authorities once it becomes profitable. Companies must then wait to be repaid. This scheme is unattractive in comparison with the legal framework generally used in the oil and gas sector. Production sharing agreements (PSA) commonly used in the international oil industry allow companies to own part of a field's oil or gas reserves, and also to share the costs and profits of its development. In this context, the Iranian BBSC system has become a key obstacle to international investment in the Iranian oil and gas sector, on top of international sanctions.

2 – The Supply Side

President Rouhani and his government carried out a process of structural reform of the country's petroleum legal framework in parallel to the international negotiations on the nuclear issue. This reflects their recognition that the lifting of international sanctions after the nuclear deal would have not been sufficient to stimulate international investment in the country's energy sector. The recently proposed Iran Petroleum Contract (IPC) is intended to combine some elements of the BBSC with some elements of the PSA, possibly allowing international companies to gain rights to a certain percentage of Iran's oil and gas reserves for 20-25 years.

The effective implementation of a new petroleum legal framework is a prerequisite for the country's comeback into global energy markets. However, neither the reform of the country's petroleum legal framework would be sufficient to pave the way for Iranian gas exports to Europe via pipeline. This simply due to energy strategy reasons internal to Iran, which might be summarized as follows.

In the short term, the hydrocarbon activities in the country will likely be focused on additional oil exploration, production and export. As Minister Zanganeh stated: «Our first priority is for enhanced oil recovery. It will be both for undeveloped and underdeveloped fields especially we prefer to start negotiations for enhanced oil recovery, for developed and existing fields.» This plan implies that in the short term even more natural gas will need to be utilized for reinjection into oil fields in order to sustain a growing oil production.

Moreover, in the short term Iran will likely make use of its natural gas resources to improve the competitiveness of its economy, through a larger share of power generation based on cheap natural gas and through further investments on CNG vehicles, in a move to reduce the domestic consumption of oil, which could thus be freed-up for additional exports.

In this overall situation, it is thus very difficult to expect major volumes of additional natural gas exports from Iran in the short term. Most probably, a volume of 10 Bcm of natural gas per year will likely represent the only additional export volume of Iran in the short term. In fact, in March 2014 Iran signed a 25-year agreement to supply

10 Bcm of natural gas per year to Oman, starting by 2017. The deal will require the construction of a 260 km-long subsea pipeline from Iran's Hormozgan Province to Oman's Sohar port on the other side of the Persian Gulf. As part of the deal, the two countries have the option of forming a joint venture to export the natural gas. This detail is not surprising, as in the past the two countries -allies since long time- have discussed several times the opportunity of bringing Iran's natural gas to Oman's underutilized LNG export facility, thus establishing Oman as a new hub for future Iranian natural gas exports. The current plan would consist in keeping about 30 percent of the natural gas exported to Oman as Iranian natural gas to be processed into LNG by Oman LNG under a tolling agreement, allowing it to market, for the very first time, what would be "Iranian LNG". This project would thus represent the first move of Iran into the global LNG markets.

In the longer term, Iran's gas resources will likely be intensively exploited with the aim to export major volumes to the international markets. At this point the question is: what will likely be the Iranian gas export strategy? Over the last decades a number of gas export projects have been discussed in Iran. At least 15 projects have been put on the table: a pipeline to Bahrain, a pipeline to Kuwait, a pipeline to the United Arab Emirates, a pipeline to Syria, a pipeline to Iraq, a pipeline to Pakistan and India, a pipeline to Europe and 7 different LNG projects.

> In the longer term, Iran's gas resources will be intensively exploited with the aim to export major volumes.

Among all these projects, over the last years Iran seemed to be particularly focused on the pipeline to Pakistan (a 22 bcm/year pipeline projected to run from Assaluyeh in Iran to Nawabshah in Southern Pakistan) also because a major share of this pipeline's capacity is devoted to supply natural gas to Iran's domestic market itself (only

8 bcm/year are supposed to be exported to Pakistan). As a matter of fact, Iran has already completed most of the 1,050 km leg from Assaluyeh to its border with Pakistan. However, this project is advancing slowly as Pakistan is not fulfilling its side of the deal (Pakistan has for some time now been unable to move ahead with its segment of the pipeline due to a serious lack of funds). After having suggested that Iran would annul its natural gas export contract with Pakistan, Oil Minister Zanganeh stated that Iran is still prepared to supply natural gas to Pakistan if it shows signs of real progress on its side of the project. Accordingly to the resolution of this issue on the Pakistani side, the Iran-Pakistan pipeline could thus be seen as a front-runner project in the future Iranian natural gas export strategy. By the way, an added value of this project is the potential for extending the pipeline to India, a country that is set to dramatically increase its natural gas consumption and import requirements after 2030. The overall project could thus well represent a major opportunity for Iran in the long term.

In parallel to this pipeline, the cornerstone of the longer-term Iranian gas strategy is certainly represented by LNG at South Pars. A substantial development of this potential might reshape global LNG markets in the post-2015 horizon, also paving the way for LNG exports from Iran to Europe. However, this project will likely advance slowly, as Iran will first need to ramp-up its gas production in order to provide the base for consistent additional natural gas exports. Such a development will require the involvement of IOCs in the country, an involvement that will unlikely occur -as previously described- without a new petroleum legal framework in the country.[23]

Figure 41. Iran gas infrastructure. Source: Central Intelligence Agency (2011).

The EU security of gas supply strategy

After the review of the existing and potential gas suppliers to Europe, we now provide a snapshot of the EU security of gas supply strategy to illustrate the growing role of EU institutions in this field also in light of the most recent policy evolutions. Security of energy supply has been for a long time a sort of unexplored area at the EU level. Only with the Green Paper "A European Strategy for Sustainable, Competitive and Secure Energy" of 2006 the EC placed security of energy supply among the three founding pillars of the EU energy policy. In particular, considering the EU's high level of dependency on external energy suppliers, the Green Paper outlined the need to ensure uninterrupted energy supply also by establishing a mechanism for rapid solidarity between Member States in the case of crisis (for instance composed by emergency oil and gas stocks) under the supervision of a European Energy Supply Observatory.

After this first step, the EC adopted in 2008 the Communication "Second Strategic Energy Review - An EU Energy Security and Solidarity Action Plan",[24] with which it proposed an Action Plan based on the following points: «1. Infrastructure needs and the diversification of energy supplies; 2. External energy relations; 3. Oil and gas stocks and crisis response mechanisms; 4. Energy efficiency; 5. Making the best use of the EU's indigenous energy resources.»[25]

This vision was further explored by the EC in 2011, with the Communication "The EU Energy Policy: Engaging with Partners beyond Our Borders",[26] an act that proposed a new strategy based on three axes: «1. Promote transparency between Member States on energy agreements with non-EU countries; 2. Help coordinate both policy toward specific partner countries and positions to be taken in international organisations; iii) Promote comprehensive energy partnerships with key partner countries.»[27]

In 2012 the European Parliament and the Council followed-up this proposal of the EC, by adopting a Decision establishing an information exchange mechanism on intergovernmental agreements between Member States and third countries in the field of energy.[28]

Finally, in 2014 the Commission adopted the Communication "European Energy Security Strategy".[29] (re)proposing a series of measures (in truth already outlined in 2008 and 2011) to tackle the EU's security of energy supply challenges such as: 1. Increase energy efficiency; 2. Increase energy production and diversify suppliers countries and routes; 3. Complete the internal energy market; 4. Speak with one voice in external energy policy; 5. Strengthen emergency and solidarity mechanisms and protect critical infrastructure.

This sizeable series of legislative activity on the issue of security of energy supply outline the growing awareness of the EU on the need for a common action on energy security. A great contribution to the inception and development of this awareness has been provided by a series of energy security crises experienced by the EU since 2006.

In particular, the Russian-Ukrainian-European gas crises of 2006 and 2009 represented a key stimulus to the EU to take an action in this field. The latest Communication adopted by the Commission in this field confirms the trend, having been launched as a response to the 2014 Ukraine crisis and the related unprecedented standoff between the EU and the Russian Federation.

However, the effectiveness of this intense legislative activity remains limited. In fact, the theoretic common approach on security of energy supply proposed by the EU continues to collide with the actual nationalist approach adopted by Member States in this field. An approach reflected by the Treaties themselves, considering that – according to Article 194 TFEU – each Member State has the right to autonomously determine its energy mix and its energy security of supply architecture.

This situation clearly elucidates that the absence of the security of energy supply element in the EU energy policy is fundamentally due to a political reason: the reluctance of Member States of ceding part of their sovereignty to the EU over an issue considered as highly strategic for their respective national interests.

In this context, it appears that only a new, strong political momentum could significantly change the situation, boosting the development of a truly European security of energy supply strategy. This is unlikely to occur in a situation of general stability, when a business-as-usual approach tends to characterize the EU (energy, but not only) policy making.

On the contrary, this might occur in a situation of urgency determined by a sudden change in the external environment, as the perception of external threats might ultimately lead the EU Member States to strengthen their union.

In the case of energy, a situation of emergency emerged again at the EU level with the 2014 Ukraine crisis.

In the case of energy, a situation of emergency emerged again at the EU level with the 2014 Ukraine crisis. In fact, the profound political rift materialized between the EU and the Russian Federation over Ukraine led to an unprecedented reconsideration of the EU-Russia energy partnership at the EU level. In that challenging situation, many European leaders called for the rapid development of a common EU strategy on security of energy supply.[30]

On the basis of an explicit request of the EU Council, the EC adopted in May 2014 the already mentioned Communication "European Energy Security Strategy", outlying the need of implementing many of the measures already proposed by the Commission itself in 2008.

However, this time the reaction of the EU was not limited to this, rather traditional, outcome. In fact, the new President of the Commission Jean-Claude Juncker announced in early September 2014 his intention to insert on its forthcoming Commission a new post for Vice President for Energy Union (in addition to the Commissioner for Energy and Climate), a move that represented a major upgrading for energy in the EU institutional structure.[31]

This move was favored also by the fact that EU leaders elected Polish Prime Minister Donald Tusk on 30 August, 2014 to be the next President of the EU Council. President Tusk expressed several times during the Ukraine crisis the need for a truly European energy policy, ultimately calling for the establishment of a European Energy Union.[32]

On this basis, the new Juncker Commission formally launched the Energy Union initiative in March 2015 with the Communication "A Framework Strategy for a Resilient Energy Union with a Forward-Looking Climate Change Policy".[33] This policy document has five interlinked parts: energy security, solidarity and trust; a fully integrated European energy market; energy efficiency contributing to moderation of demand; decarbonisation of the economy; and research, innovation and competitiveness.

Given the origins of the document it is no surprise that energy security is mentioned first. According to the document, energy security should be safeguarded by reducing energy consumption, strengthening the internal exchange of energy and diversifying energy supplies. While reducing consumption and improving energy markets relate to the second and third parts of the Energy Union (internal market and energy efficiency), diversification measures are seen as the core of energy security. To diversify the sources of Europe's gas imports, the EC basically reiterates the need for further action on the two, usual, gas security policy lines:

1. To reinforce partnerships with current and perspective gas producing and transit countries. The Communication clearly mentions traditional suppliers such as Algeria and Norway but also perspective transit countries such as Turkey. This latest is mentioned in relation to the Southern Gas Corridor, the importance of which is outlined in the Communication in a very clear way.

2. To enhance the role of LNG in the European gas market by promoting more interconnections within the EU but also a better synergy between LNG and storage. In early 2016 the EC made a step forward in the advancement of this policy line by defining the missing links within the EU that will need to be realized to effectively allow LNG to play a greater role in the system (Figure 42).

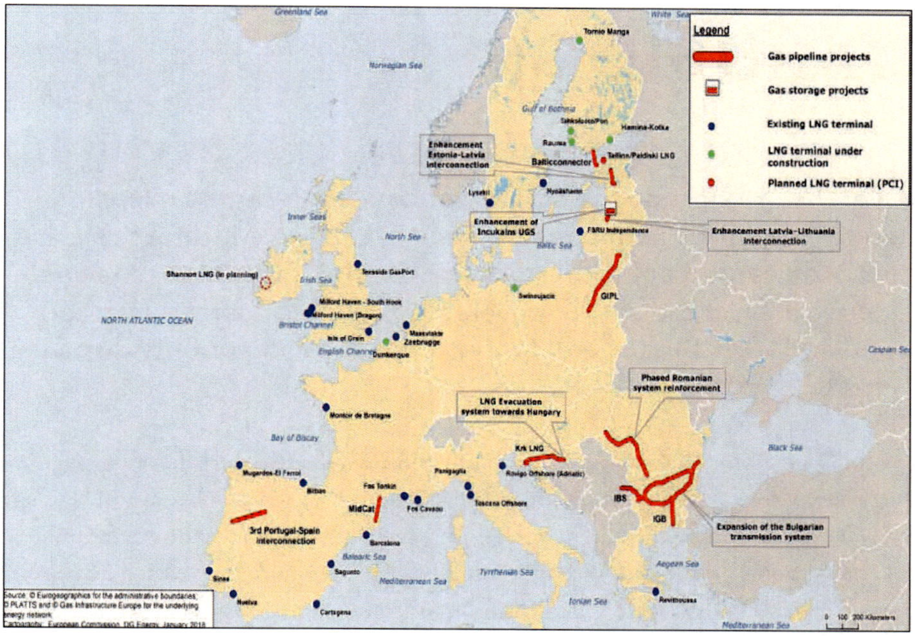

Figure 42. EU infrastructure relevant for the LNG strategy. Source: EC (2016).

Conclusions

Over the last decade the EU has certainly represented a leading force of the global fight against climate change. Much of this effort has been carried out with a focus on the deployment of renewable energy, even at the cost of developing variable sources such as wind and PV with a "fit and forget" logic entailing priority dispatch and access to network.

To continue along its decarbonisation path, the EU will need in the future even more variable renewables into the system. This will require profound changes in terms of power system operation, market design, infrastructure development, transformation of conventional generation mix and demand side management policies. To make a long story short, in order to achieve its climate targets the EU will need to rethink its energy system beyond renewable energy itself.

Among the various possible options of conventional electricity generation (gas, coal, nuclear and oil), gas seems to be the fuel better placed to play a key complementary role to renewable energy in the decarbonisation path for the following four reasons:

1. Gas-fired power plants can provide the flexible back-up capacity needed in a system with high share of variable renewable energy sources;

2. By displacing coal in the EU electricity generation systems gas has the potential to generate immediate and substantial GHG emissions' reductions;

3. A switch from coal-fired power plants to gas-fired power plants will not only positively impact the EU environmental effort at macro level but also at micro level. In fact, compared with coal and oil, gas avoids or reduces much of the local environmental damage arising from fossil-fuel use;

4. Gas can also play a role in the decarbonising the transport sector, not only in terms of compressed gas vehicles, but also in terms of LNG for trucks and for ships.

Considering these elements, gas might thus well play an important role in the future EU decarbonisation path. For this reason it is important to explore the outlook for EU gas production, consumption and import requirements in order to understand the challenges and opportunities that might arise in the future. Our analysis illustrated that over the next decades the EU domestic gas production will continue its downward trajectory, thus increasing the EU import requirements even in strong decarbonisation scenarios. This feature unveils the structural nature of the EU dependency on external gas suppliers, outlining the importance of the security of gas supply issue.

While discussing EU security of gas supply, it is impossible to avoid the issue of EU-Russia gas relations – particularly after the 2014 Ukraine crisis. After those events, the EU-Russia gas relations have basically assisted to a two, opposite, trends. On the one hand cooperation between Gazprom and European companies continued. On the other hand, the EU-Russia gas partnership has remained frozen at the institutional level, with no signs of rapprochement. This situation not only signals the different approaches being adopted *vis-à-vis* Russia by the EU institutions and European oil and gas companies, but also the different political stances in the field of the EU institutions and of certain EU Member States. Notwithstadning the political difficulties, the EU-Russia gas relations will most likely continue in business-as-usual also due to the clear interdependece between the two parties in the sector. In short, Europe needs Russian gas as well as Russia needs the European market. This 'unavoidable' cooperation is also consolidated by the fact that the EU and Russia are linked by long-term contracts guaranteeing the delivery of at least 80 bcm of Russian gas to Europe in 2025.

On the contrary of Russia, the other two key pipeline suppliers to Europe enjoy good relations with the EU but face different challenges as far as their production and export outlooks are concerned. On the one hand, Norway has always been a reliable gas supplier to the EU, but some concerns are emerging about its capability to deliver its gas supply in the long-term. In fact, according to the Norwegian Petroleum Directorate, the country's gas production will peak around 2020 and then progressively decline. Though there is uncertainty on future potential discoveries, which could significantly delay this decline. On the other hand, Algeria is facing both geological and political challenges. In fact, the recent downgrade of the country's gas reserve estimation adds concerns about the sustainability of the country's production and export performances, on top of the already serious institutional and governance bottlenecks ranging from the paralysis of the country political decision making due to the uncertain conditions of the President, to the key unresolved issues of energy subsidies and unattractiveness of the petroleum legal framework. The current low oil price environment could well provide a good opportunity for the country to make necessary reforms in the field. Furthermore, it should also be outlined that a major opportunity for the country might be the development of the shale gas resources that are estimated to be among the highest in the world.

With regard to LNG, a major wave is on the horizon. In fact, a vast expansion of LNG exports in the period up to 2025 is expected, as a result of the major capacity addition (from Australia to the United States) that characterizes the period 2015-2020. This expanding cycle will have a strong impact on the LNG market over the next years, also in terms of pricing. In fact, gas importers are expected to benefit from this situation as growing supply will put a downward pressure on prices all over the world. However, this favourable situation for LNG importers might well revers in the 2020s, with a new cycle of tighter markets resulting from delayed investment in new LNG projects due to low prices in the period 2015-2020.

To focus on the prospects for Europe in the period up to 2020, it is possible to expect that dropping LNG prices will strongly affect the overall structure of European gas markets. In fact, the availability of low-cost LNG will put pressure on gas producers such as Russia, Algeria and Norway, which will have to decide on whether to defend its existing pricing formulae or defend its market share by competing with LNG suppliers. This is particularly true if considering that about 150 bcm of gas import contracts to the EU are set to expire over the next ten years. As previously mentioned, Russia is contractually well protected by 2025 against the massive wave of LNG expected to materialize in the second half of the present decade. Moreover, Russia will most likely be committed to export to Europe much more than the minimum contracted quantities and for this reason Gazprom has already announced that it will fight for market share in Europe. Therefore, it is well possible to expect a future price war in Europe with LNG competing with Russian gas at spot basis.

Europe not only has a well-established LNG infrastructure, but this is also currently strongly under-utilized at the impressive level of 68 percent (or 124 bcm, a level corresponding to Russia's gas exports to the EU), thus providing a huge margin for additional LNG imports. This large under-utilization does not, however, imply that all these volumes could concretely be brought where needed in the EU. In fact, interconnections and reverse flows systems are still missing among various EU member states, creating a physical limit to the exploitation of the continent's LNG potential. For this reason, the creation of a truly interconnected and flexible EU gas market is to be considered as a key priority for the EU.

After the discovery of the Zohr field, Egypt seems to hold the keys of the Eastern Mediterranean gas future. In fact, it might opt to develop its resources in parallel to Israel and Cyprus, by creating a new Eastern Mediterranean gas hub based on its existing exporting infrastructure. Albeit commercially soundly, the realization of such a development will ultimately depend on geopolitical factors. In particular, this will depend on the political willingness of Egypt and Israel to cooperate in such a highly strategic sector.

Over the last two decades, the Southern Gas Corridor has represented a key topic of any discussion concerning the EU gas security of supply. However, the 10 bcm/year by 2019 of Azerbaijan are the only tangible input that this initiative will provide to EU gas markets in the foreseeable future. In fact, none of the other potential suppliers in the region (Turkmenistan, Iraq, Iran) are likely to join Azerbaijan in this initiative anytime soon.

Conclusions

With the launch of the Energy Union initiative in March 2015, security of gas supply surged at the top of the EU energy agenda. According to the new policy package, energy security should be safeguarded by reducing energy consumption, strengthening the internal exchange of energy and diversifying energy supplies. Such an holistic approach is more than welcome. In fact, as the book tried to illustrate, many are the challenges and opportunities characterizing the European climate and energy policy in general and the European gas policy in particular. Only by adopting a wider perspective able to see trade-offs and complementarities of various policy actions a sustainable way forward could effectively be pursued. The wish of the authors is that the European policy makers will be able to address the many still-open questions of the EU decarbonisation path, to secure its future sustainability for the benefit of all.

With the launch of the Energy Union initiative in March 2015, security of gas supply surged at the top of the EU energy agenda.

Notes

1 Platts (2014), *Dutch Groningen gas field output cut to 42.5 Bcm in 2014, 2015,* 14 January, available online.

2 Reuters (2015), *Dutch government sets 2015/2016 Groningen gas production at 27 Bcm,* 18 December, available online.

3 Reuters (2015), *Dutch to sharply cut Groningen gas production,* 18 December, available online.

4 UK Department of Energy and Climate Change (2014), *UKCS Oil and Gas Production Projections,* available online.

5 For a multisciplinary analysis of shale gas in the EU refer to: Musialski, C., Zittel, W., Lechtenböhmer, S., Altmann, M. (eds.) (2013), *Shale Gas in Europe,* Claeys and Casteels, Deventer.

6 The Guardian (2015), *Polish shale industry collapsing as number of licenses nearly halves,* 9 October, available online.

7 As described in the IEA official page: http://www.iea.org/publications/scenariosandprojections/

8 *Ibidem.*

9 Energy Intelligence (2014), "Russia Cancels South Stream Project, Plans to Redirect Volumes to Turkey", December 2.

10 Energy Intelligence (2015), "Gazprom Agrees Turk Stream Land Route", February 12.

11 The remaining 49 Bcm/y would then be available on the border with Greece for purchase by European customers after other three legs are built. The timing of this second phase was far more uncertain than the first one, also considering the need of reviewing or signing new long-term contracts between Gazprom and its European customers (at least the new delivery points need to be agreed by the Parties) and building pipeline connections across the Balkans to evacuate the gas from the Turkish-Greek border to the core European gas markets.

12 There is a major uncertainty regarding the factual size of the country's conventional gas reserves. For instance, they are estimated at 2 tcm by Wood Mackenzie.

13 International Energy Agency (2015), *World Energy Outlook 2015,* OECD, Paris.

14 IEA (2015).

15 Cedigaz (2015)

16 Heather, P. (2015), *The Evolution of European Traded Gas Hubs,* NG 104, Oxford Institute for Energy Studies, Oxford.

17 Not only because of the investments already made on its Shah Deniz natural gas field, but also because of the need to reach a final investment decision for Shah Deniz Phase II (a decision that finally arrived on December 17, 2013).

18 "Nabucco-West: Abridged Pipeline Project Officially Submitted to Shah Deniz Consortium", in *Eurasia Daily Monitor,* Vol. 9, Issue 98, 23 May 2012.

19 European Commission, *Commissioner Oettinger welcomes decision on "Nabucco West" pipeline,* Press Release, 28 June 2012. The Nabucco West project was also supported by British Petroleum (BP), the operator of Shah Deniz Phase II. In fact, in order to support Nabucco West, in June 2012 BP ceased the development of its South East Europe Pipeline (SEEP), a project launched in September 2011 to carry the TANAP 10 bcm/year destined to Europe from the Turkish-European border to Austria.

Notes

20 "Shah Deniz consortium chooses TAP to carry Azeri gas to Europe", in *Reuters,* 28 June 2013. Nabucco West also had the support of British Petroleum. In September 2011 British Petroleum also proposed a pipeline project, the so-called South East Europe Pipeline (SEEP), to carry the TANAP 10 bcm/year destined to Europe from the Turkish-European border to Austria. Albeit designed by the operator of Shah Deniz Phase II .

21 The TAP project was announced in 2003 by Swiss energy company EGL Group. The feasibility study was concluded in March 2006. Two options were investigated: a northern route through Bulgaria, Republic of Macedonia and Albania, and a southern route through Greece and Albania, which finally was considered to be more feasible.

22 For a detailed discussion of Turkmenistan's natural gas market please refer to: Pirani, S. (2012), *Central Asian and Caspian Gas Production and the Constraints on Export,* OIES Paper: NG 69, Oxford Institute for Energy Studies.

23 For a detailed discussion of the future prospects of Iran's natural gas market please refer to: Tagliapietra, S. (2014), *Iran after the (potential) nuclear deal. What's next for the country's natural gas market?,* Nota di Lavoro n. 31.2014, Fondazione Eni Enrico Mattei.

24 *Second Strategic Energy Review - An EU Energy Security and Solidarity Action Plan,* Communication from the Commission to the European Parliament and the Council, COM(2008) 781.

25 *Ibidem,* p. 5.

26 *The EU Energy Policy: Engaging with Partners beyond Our Borders,* Communication from the Commission to the European Parliament, the Council, the European Economic and Social Committee and the Committee on the Regions, COM(2011) 539 final.

27 *Ibidem,* p. 15.

28 Decision No 994/2012/EU of 25 October 2012 establishing an information exchange mechanism with regard to intergovernmental agreements between Member States and third countries in the field of energy.

29 *European Energy Security Strategy,* Communication from the Commission to the European Parliament, the Council, the European Economic and Social Committee and the Committee on the Regions, COM(2014) 330 final.

30 European Council, Conclusions, EUCO 7/1/14 REV1, 29/21 March 2014.

31 *EurActiv, The Juncker team revealed,* September 4, 2014.

32 Donald Tusk, *A united Europe can end Russia's energy stronghold,* Financial Times, April 21, 2014.

33 European Commission (2015), *A Framework Strategy for a Resilient Energy Union with a Forward-Looking Climate Change Policy,* COM(2015) 80 final.

Appendix

Appendix

Commision Communication COM/2015/080 final of 25 February 2015 – A Framework Strategy for a Resilient Energy Union with a Forward-Looking Climate Change Policy,

Appendix

Energy Union Package

A Framework Strategy for a Resilient Energy Union with a Forward-Looking Climate Change Policy

Communication from the Commission to the European Parliament, the Council, the European Economic and Social Committee of the regions and the European Investment bank

COM(2015) 80 final, 25.2.2015

1. WHY WE NEED AN ENERGY UNION

The goal of a resilient Energy Union with an ambitious climate policy at its core is to give EU consumers - households and businesses - secure, sustainable, competitive and affordable energy. Achieving this goal will require a fundamental transformation of Europe's energy system.

Our vision is of an Energy Union where Member States see that they depend on each other to deliver secure energy to their citizens, based on true solidarity and trust, and of an Energy Union that speaks with one voice in global affairs;
Our vision is of an integrated continent-wide energy system where energy flows freely across borders, based on competition and the best possible use of resources, and with effective regulation of energy markets at EU level where necessary;

Our vision is of the Energy Union as a sustainable, low-carbon and climate-friendly economy that is designed to last;

Our vision is of strong, innovative and competitive European companies that develop the industrial products and technology needed to deliver energy efficiency and low carbon technologies inside and outside Europe,

Our vision is of a European labour force with the skills to build and manage the energy system of tomorrow;

Our vision is of investor confidence through price signals that reflect long term needs and policy objectives;

Most importantly, our vision is of an Energy Union with citizens at its core, where citizens take ownership of the energy transition, benefit from new technologies to reduce their bills, participate actively in the market, and where vulnerable consumers are protected.

To reach our goal, we have to move away from an economy driven by fossil fuels, an economy where energy is based on a centralised, supply-side approach and which relies on old technologies and outdated business models. We have to empower consumers through providing them with information, choice and through creating flexibility to manage demand as well as supply. We have to move away from a fragmented system characterised by uncoordinated national policies, market barriers and energy-isolated areas.

European energy system in figures

Latest data shows that the EU imported 53% of its energy at a cost of around EUR 400 billion, which makes it the largest energy importer in the world. Six Member States depend on a single external supplier for their entire gas imports and therefore remain too vulnerable to supply shocks. It has also been estimated that every additional 1% increase in energy savings cuts gas imports by 2.6%.[1] 75% of our housing stock is energy inefficient. 94% percent of transport relies on oil products, of which 90% is imported. Collectively, the EU spent over EUR 120 billion per year - directly or indirectly - on energy subsidies, often not justified.[2] Over EUR 1 trillion need to be invested into the energy sector in EU by 2020 alone.[3]

Wholesale electricity prices for European countries are at low levels, though still 30% higher than in the US. At the same time, post-tax electricity prices for households increased on average by 4.4% from 2012 to 2013. Wholesale gas prices are still more than twice as high as in the US[4]. The price difference with other economies has an impact on the competitiveness of our industry, in particular our energy-intensive industries.

European renewable energy businesses have a combined annual turnover of €129bn and employ over a million people[5]. EU companies have a share of 40% of all patents for renewable technologies.[6] The challenge is to retain Europe's leading role in global investment in renewable energy.[7]

Today, the European Union has energy rules set at the European level, but in practice it has 28 national regulatory frameworks. This cannot continue. An integrated energy market is needed to create more competition, lead to greater market efficiency through better use of energy generation facilities across the EU and to produce affordable prices for consumers.

The retail market is not functioning properly. Many household consumers have too little choice of energy suppliers and too little control over their energy costs. An unacceptably high percentage of European households cannot afford to pay their energy bills.

Energy infrastructure is ageing and not adjusted to the increased production from renewables. There is a need to attract investments, but the current market design and national policies do not set the right incentives and provide insufficient predictability for potential investors.

Energy islands continue to exist as many markets are not properly connected to their neighbours. This adds to the costs faced by consumers and creates vulnerability in terms of energy security.

We are still leaders in innovation and renewable energy, but other parts of the world are fast catching up and we have already lost ground when it comes to some clean, low carbon technologies.

Building up investment in high-tech, globally competing companies through stable policies will bring jobs and growth to Europe. New business sectors, new business models and new job profiles will emerge. Such transformational change profoundly affects the roles of all actors in the energy system, including the consumers.

Europe needs to make the right choices now. If it continues on the present path, the unavoidable challenge of shifting to a low-carbon economy will be made harder by the economic, social and environmental costs of having fragmented national energy markets. The current low oil and gas prices, while they last, should be seized as an historic opportunity - when combined with the falling cost of cleaner forms of energy, a strong EU climate policy and the emergence of new technologies - to reset the EU's energy policy in the right direction: that of an Energy Union.

2. THE WAY FORWARD

The Energy Union strategy has five mutually-reinforcing and closely interrelated dimensions designed to bring greater energy security, sustainability and competitiveness:

- Energy security, solidarity and trust;
- A fully integrated European energy market;
- Energy efficiency contributing to moderation of demand;
- Decarbonising the economy, and
- Research, Innovation and Competitiveness

2.1. Energy security, solidarity and trust

In May 2014 the Commission set out in its Energy Security Strategy[8] how the EU remains vulnerable to external energy shocks and called on policy makers at national and EU level to make clear to citizens the choices involved in reducing our dependency on particular fuels, energy suppliers and routes. The Energy Union builds on this strategy.

The key drivers of energy security are the completion of the internal energy market and more efficient energy consumption. It depends on more transparency as well as on more solidarity and trust between the Member States. The EU's energy security is closely linked with its neighbours.

Joint approaches in the field of energy can make all parts of the European Union stronger, for instance in case of supply shortages or disruptions. The spirit of solidarity in energy matters is explicitly mentioned in the Treaty and is at the heart of the Energy Union.

Diversification of supply (energy sources, suppliers and routes)

The political challenges over the last months have shown that diversification of energy sources, suppliers and routes is crucial for ensuring secure and resilient energy supplies to European citizens and companies, who expect access to affordable and competitively priced energy at any given moment. To ensure the diversification in gas supplies, work on the Southern Gas Corridor must be intensified to enable Central Asian countries to export their gas to Europe. In Northern Europe, the establishment of liquid gas hubs with multiple suppliers is greatly enhancing supply security. This example should be followed in Central and Eastern Europe, and in the Mediterranean area, where a Mediterranean gas hub is in the making.

Constructing the infrastructure to deliver new sources of gas to the EU involves many partners, and is both complex and expensive. Resolving these issues requires resolute action at EU level. The Commission will reinforce its support for this process through the use of all available Community funding instruments in particular the future European Fund for Strategic Investments (EFSI), and fully involving European financial institutions. However, the necessary infrastructure must also be in place inside the EU, including the possibility of reverse flows, to bring the gas to where it is needed.

We will explore the full potential of liquefied natural gas (LNG), including as a back-up in crisis situations when insufficient gas is coming into Europe through the existing pipeline system. Increases in LNG trade will help to bring world natural gas prices closer together. LNG prices have over recent years been higher compared to pipeline gas due in particular to high liquefaction, regasification and transportation costs and demand in Asia. In order to address these issues, the Commission will prepare a comprehensive LNG strategy, which will also look into the necessary transport infrastructure linking LNG access points with the internal market. The potential of gas storage in Europe and the regulatory framework needed to ensure sufficient gas in storage for winter will also be addressed in this context. The Commission will also work to remove obstacles to LNG imports from the US and other LNG producers.

Given the EU's import dependence and global climate change challenges, we need to take additional measures to reduce its oil consumption. Oil prices are currently low because of excess production, combined with lower consumption and increased energy efficiency.[9]

The EU is highly dependent on the import of nuclear fuel and related services to Member States where nuclear energy is part of the energy mix. Diversification of supply is important to ensure security of supply. The Commission will update and enhance the requirements on the information to be provided, in accordance with Article 41 of the Euratom Treaty, on nuclear installation projects.

Domestically produced energy also contributes to decreasing Europe's energy import dependence. This includes notably renewables, needed for decarbonisation, as well as conventional and - for those Member States that choose it - non-conventional fossil resources. Producing oil and gas from unconventional sources in Europe such as shale gas is an option, provided that issues of public acceptance and environmental impact are adequately addressed.

Working together on security of supply

Member States, transmission system operators, the energy industry and all other stakeholders have to work closely together to ensure a high-level of energy security for European citizens and companies.

Regarding oil, important steps have been taken already with the adoption of the 2009 Oil Stocks Directive.[10] which foresees obligations for Member States to build up and maintain minimum stocks of crude oil and petroleum products.

Member States should be assured that in situations of tight supply, they can rely on their neighbours. The Commission's 2014 Report on short-term resilience in the gas sector[11] stressed the need for stronger cooperation in responding to a potential supply disruption. To introduce common crisis management, the Commission will propose preventive and emergency plans at regional and EU level, including the

Energy Community contracting parties. Solidarity among Member States, in particular in times of supply crisis, has to be strengthened. These issues and the experience gained in the implementation of the Regulation will be taken into account when proposing a revision of the Security of Gas Supply Regulation.

The Commission will assess options for voluntary demand aggregation mechanisms for collective purchasing of gas during a crisis and where Member States are dependent on a single supplier. This would need to be fully compliant with WTO rules and EU competition rules.

Many Member States currently have inadequate security of electricity supply frameworks in place and they use outdated and inconsistent approaches to assessing security of electricity supply. Working together with Member States, the Commission will establish a range of acceptable risk levels for supply interruptions, and an objective, EU-wide, fact-based security of supply assessment addressing the situation in Member States. This will take into account cross-border flows, variable renewable production, demand response and storage possibilities. Capacity mechanisms should only be developed to address security of supply if a regional system adequacy assessment points to such a need, taking into account the potential for energy efficiency and demand-side response.[12]

Stronger European role in global energy markets

The Energy Union is not an inward-looking project. A stronger and more united EU can engage more constructively with its partners, to their mutual benefit.

Energy policy is often used as a foreign policy tool, in particular in major energy producing and transit countries. This reality has to be taken into account when discussing Europe's external energy policy. Therefore, the European Union has to improve its ability to project its weight on global energy markets. Together with its major partners, the European Union will work towards an improved global governance system for energy, leading to more competitive and transparent global energy markets.

EU trade policy contributes to greater energy security and diversification through the inclusion of energy-related provisions in trade agreements with its partners. Where the EU negotiates agreements with countries that are important from a security of supply perspective, the Commission will seek as a priority to negotiate energy specific provisions contributing to the energy security, notably access to resources, and sustainable energy goals of the Energy Union. In general, the Commission will pursue an active trade and investment agenda in the energy field, including access to foreign markets for European energy technology and services.[13]

As part of a revitalised European energy and climate diplomacy, the EU will use all its foreign policy instruments to establish strategic energy partnerships with increasingly important producing and transit countries or regions such as Algeria and Turkey; Azerbaijan and Turkmenistan; the Middle East; Africa and other potential suppliers.

The EU will further develop its partnership with Norway, the EU's second largest supplier of crude oil and natural gas. The EU will continue to integrate Norway fully into its internal energy policies. The EU will also develop its partnerships with countries such as the United States and Canada.

When the conditions are right, the EU will consider reframing the energy relationship with Russia based on a level playing field in terms of market opening, fair competition, environmental protection and safety, for the mutual benefit of both sides.
Particular attention will be paid to upgrading the Strategic Partnership on energy with Ukraine. This will address issues related to Ukraine's importance as a transit country as well as those related to Ukraine's energy market reforms, such as the upgrade of its gas network, the setting up of an appropriate regulatory framework for the electricity market and increasing energy efficiency in Ukraine as a means of reducing its dependence on imported energy.

In our immediate neighbourhood, the Commission will propose to strengthen the Energy Community, ensuring effective implementation of the EU's energy, environment and competition acquis, energy market reforms and incentivising investments in the energy sector. The goal is closer integration of the EU and Energy Community energy markets. The energy relationships with the European Neighbourhood Partnership (ENP) countries will be considered in the ongoing ENP review.

More transparency on gas supply

An important element in ensuring energy (and in particular gas) security is full compliance of agreements related to the buying of energy from third countries with EU law. Such compliance checks for Intergovernmental Agreements (IGAs) and related commercial agreements based on the relevant Decision[14] are currently carried out after a Member State and a third country have concluded an agreement. In practice, we have seen that renegotiating such agreements is very difficult. The positions of the signatories have already been fixed, which creates political pressure not to change any aspect of the agreement. In future, the Commission should be informed about the negotiation of intergovernmental agreements from an early stage, so that a better ex ante assessment of IGA's compatibility with internal market rules and security of supply criteria is ensured. Commission participation in such negotiations with third countries and a move towards standard contract clauses could also more effectively avoid undue pressure and ensure respect of European rules. Therefore, the Commission will review the Intergovernmental Agreements Decision and will propose options to ensure that the EU speaks with one voice in negotiations with third countries.

In the context of the review of the Security of Gas Supply Regulation, the Commission will also propose to ensure appropriate transparency of commercial gas supply contracts that may have an impact on EU energy security, while safeguarding the confidentiality of sensitive information.

2.2. A fully-integrated internal energy market

Despite progress made in recent years, Europe's energy system is still underperforming. The current market design does not lead to sufficient investments, market concentration and weak competition remain an issue and the European energy landscape is still too fragmented. We have to give a new political boost to completing the internal energy market.

The internal market's hardware: connecting markets through interconnections

At this moment, the European electricity and gas transmission systems, notably cross-border connections, are not sufficient to make the internal energy market work properly and to link the remaining energy islands to the main electricity and gas network.

Work on infrastructure projects has accelerated in recent years, even more so in light of recent events at the European Union's Eastern border. In 2013, the European Union identified 248 energy infrastructure Projects of Common Interest (PCIs). The list will be reviewed and up-dated later this year and then again every other year.[15] In 2014, the European Energy Security Strategy identified 33 infrastructure projects which are essential to improve security of supply and better connect energy markets. A specific minimum interconnection target has been set for electricity at 10% of installed electricity production capacity of the Member States, which should be achieved by 2020. The necessary measures to achieve this 10% target are set out in the Commission Communication presented with this Energy Union Strategic Framework. In 2016, the Commission will report on the necessary measures to reach a 15% target by 2030.

The transition towards a more secure and sustainable energy system will require major investments in generation, networks and energy efficiency, estimated at some € 200 billion annually in the next decade.[16] While the private sector will bear the costs of much of these investments, access to financing will be key. Today, the European Investment Bank, the Connecting Europe Facility and financing under the European Structural and Investment Funds already provide the means. Moreover, the proposed European Fund for Strategic Investments will provide additional support, hence, further facilitating access to finance for projects of European significance such as in energy networks, renewable energy and energy efficiency. The Commission will explore proposals for energy investment regimes that pool resources to finance economically viable investments, avoiding market distortion and fragmentation.

Investors can draw on the Investment Portal being set up as part of the European Fund for Strategic Investments that is designed to boost the transparency of the EU investment project pipeline to make information accessible to potential investors. The Commission will also bring together information on infrastructure projects funded by the Connecting Europe Facility and EU Cohesion Policy Funds, to bring more coherence in the wide array of existing funding schemes and maximise their impact. The Commission will regularly take stock of the implementation of major infrastructure projects which contribute to the Energy Union, in particular in the framework of the PCI follow-up. As part of this stock-taking exercise, it will make an annual report on the progress to reach the 10% electricity interconnection target with a specific focus on the implementation of the regional action plans. Finally, the Commission will also convene a dedicated Energy Infrastructure Forum where progress should be discussed with the Member States, relevant regional cooperation groups as well as with EU institutions. It will meet for the first time in late 2015.

Implementing and upgrading the internal energy market's software

Full implementation and strict enforcement of existing energy and related legislation is the first priority to establish the Energy Union. There is no point in developing new policies and approaches on weak foundations.

The Commission will use all available policy instruments in this regard and will insist that Member States fully implement and enforce the 3rd Internal Energy Market Package, in particular as regards unbundling and the independence of regulators. Certain ex-ante conditions must be met so that the European Structural and Investment Funds can be used for co-financing energy investments. This will help to ensure compliance with EU energy legislation.

Strict enforcement of the Treaty's competition rules will help to prevent companies from distorting the internal energy market. Antitrust enforcement will ensure that energy can flow freely by addressing territorial restrictions in supply contracts as well as upstream/downstream and network foreclosure issues (including interconnectors). The Commission will also assess – through competition law enforcement – the evolution and formation of energy prices.

A well-functioning internal energy market needs an effective regulatory framework. The 3rd Internal Energy Market Package set up bodies to ensure cooperation among transmission system operators and regulators. In the context of the market design discussion, the functioning of these bodies will be strengthened. Currently decisions in these bodies still reflect national views.

Transmission system operation will need to become much more integrated to meet the challenges of the transformed energy system. The European Networks of Transmission System Operators for Electricity and Gas (ENTSO-E/G), which were also set-up by the 3rd Internal Energy Market Package, need to be upgraded to fulfil such a role. Regional operational centres will have to be created, so that they can effectively plan and manage cross-border electricity and gas flows.

The Agency for Cooperation of Energy Regulators (ACER) was established by the 3rd Internal Energy Market Package to assist national regulators, in particular on cross-border issues. However, ACER currently acts primarily through recommendations and opinions. It has very limited decision-making rights, e.g. it can only take decisions at the request of the national regulators or if they fail to take a decision within a certain timeframe. EU-wide regulation of the single market should be strengthened, through a significant reinforcement of the powers and independence of ACER to carry out regulatory functions at the European level in order to enable it to effectively oversee the development of the internal energy market and the related market rules as well as to deal with all cross-border issues necessary to create a seamless internal market.[17]

The 3rd Internal Energy Market Package also provided for the adoption of network codes in order to help harmonise the flow of electricity and gas across different transmission systems. This work has to be completed to ensure a better functioning of cross-border energy markets.

Market integration of renewable electricity generation requires flexible markets, both on the supply and demand side, within and beyond a Member State's borders. Electricity grids must therefore evolve significantly. There is a need to expand the possibilities for distributed generation and demand-side management, including intraday markets, to develop new high-voltage long distance connections (super-grids) and new storage technologies.

The Commission will prepare an ambitious legislative proposal to redesign the electricity market and linking wholesale and retail. This will increase security of supply and ensure that the electricity market will be better adapted to the energy transition which will bring in a multitude of new producers, in particular of renewable energy sources, as well as enable full participation of consumers in the market notably through demand response. Closer integration, including on a regional level, more cross-border trade and the development of both short and long term markets with effective price formation will deliver the right investment signals as well as the necessary flexibility to allow market integration of new generation sources.

A fully functioning internal energy market, providing efficient investment signals, is the best means to reduce the need for capacity mechanisms. The Commission has already set out guidance[18] and rules[19] to limit the detrimental effects of badly-designed, fragmented and uncoordinated public interventions. However, effective application of this guidance can only be a first step to ensure that divergent national market arrangements, such as capacity mechanisms and uncoordinated renewables support schemes become more compatible with the internal market.[20] Even though in some cases required and justified to address market failures, some forms of public intervention have had a serious negative impact on the effective functioning of the internal energy market. The Commission will work together with Member States to ensure that capacity mechanisms and support for renewable electricity are fully in line with existing rules and do not distort the internal energy market. Environmentally harmful subsidies need to be phased out altogether.[21] A reformed Emission Trading System will also play an important role in setting the right investment signals. Finally, the Commission will ensure greater transparency in the composition of energy costs and prices by developing regular and detailed monitoring and reporting, including on impacts of energy costs and prices on competitiveness. Particular attention will be paid to public interventions such as regulated tariffs, energy taxation policies and the level of public support, as well as their impact on pricing mechanisms, including electricity tariff deficits.

Enhanced regional cooperation within a common EU framework

In an Energy Union, Member States must coordinate and cooperate with their neighbours when developing their energy policies.

Technical implementation of the different elements of our Energy Union strategy will be very complex. Some elements, such as new market arrangements for short term markets in gas and electricity or integrating the operations of transmission system operators should be developed and implemented at regional level as a step towards full EU-wide market integration. Existing arrangements such as the Pentalateral Energy Forum or the Baltic Energy Market Interconnection Plan (BEMIP) are initiatives on which to build further. Successes in these regions should act as a catalyst for other regions. The Commission will ensure that all regional initiatives evolve in a coherent way and lead towards a fully integrated Single Energy Market.

Given its particular vulnerability, there is a need to improve cooperation, solidarity and trust in the Central and South-Eastern part of Europe. Dedicated cooperation arrangements would help to accelerate the better integration of these markets into the wider European energy market which would improve the liquidity and resilience of the energy system and would allow full use of the region's energy efficiency and renewable energy potential. The Commission will take concrete initiatives in this regard as an urgent priority.

For the Northern and Baltic Seas, the Commission will work with Member States and industry on delivering cost-reduction to these offshore energy systems.

A new deal for consumers

In an Energy Union, consumers in one Member State should be able to make informed choices and buy their energy freely and simply from a company in another Member State. This requires the further adaptation of the current national regulatory frameworks since the vast majority of European households remain passive consumers. In some Member States consumers have a limited choice of suppliers and switching between suppliers is relatively cumbersome.

In order to empower consumers, Member States and their authorities need to fully implement and enforce existing European rules, including consumer protection rules. Necessary support measures should be undertaken also by regional and local authorities, so that consumers have understandable, readily-accessible information, user-friendly tools, and financial incentives for saving energy.

Smart technologies will help consumers and energy service companies working for them to reap the opportunities available on the energy market by taking control of their energy consumption (and possible self-production). This will deliver more flexibility in the market and potentially reduce consumer bills.

The Commission will continue to push for standardisation and to support the national roll-out of smart meters[22] and to promote the further development of smart appliances and smart grids, so that flexible energy use is rewarded. It will develop synergies between the Energy Union and the Digital Single Market agenda and take measures to ensure privacy protection and cyber-security.

However, this will only work if market prices send the right signals. In a number of Member States, regulated tariffs still limit the development of effective competition, which discourages investments and the emergence of new market players.

Regulated end-user prices are often used to protect households or even non-household customers from increases in energy costs. The impact of such measures falls on non-regulated customers, on electricity companies and/or public finances, where electricity tariff deficits are incurred. However, in the long run, these measures harm the interests of the consumers they are meant to help. The Commission will seek the phasing-out of below cost regulated prices through the competition and economic governance frameworks. It will also encourage Member States to establish a road map for the phasing-out of all regulated prices.

Protecting vulnerable consumers

Energy poverty negatively affects living conditions and health. It has many causes, mostly resulting from a combination of low income and general poverty conditions, inefficient homes and a housing tenure system that fails to encourage energy efficiency. Energy poverty can only be tackled by a combination of measures, mainly in the social field and within the competence of authorities on the national, regional or local levels. When phasing out regulated prices, Member States need to propose a mechanism to protect vulnerable consumers, which could preferably be provided through the general welfare system. If provided through the energy market, it could be implemented through schemes such as a solidarity tariff or as a discount on energy bills. The cost of such schemes needs to be covered by non-eligible consumers collectively. Hence, it is important that such a system is well targeted to keep overall costs low and to limit the distortions deriving from regulated prices (e.g. not increase further tariff deficits in Member States).

2.3. Energy efficiency as a contribution to the moderation of energy demand

The European Council set in October 2014 an indicative target at the EU level of at least 27% for improving energy efficiency in 2030. This will be reviewed by 2020, having in mind an EU level of 30%. It is in this context necessary to fundamentally rethink energy efficiency and treat it as an energy source in its own right, representing the value of energy saved. As part of the market design review, the Commission will ensure that energy efficiency and demand side response can compete on equal terms with generation capacity.

Most of the work has to be done at national, regional and local level, but the Commission can play a strong role creating the appropriate framework for progress. The Commission will, therefore, encourage Member States to give energy efficiency primary consideration in their policies.

The EU has already put in place the world's leading set of measures to become more efficient in our energy consumption. Through energy labelling and ecodesign legislation, consumers can make informed energy consumption choices. While all economic sectors must take steps to increase the efficiency of their energy consumption, the Commission will pay special attention to those sectors with a huge energy efficiency potential, in particular the transport and buildings sector. The Commission will further establish synergies between energy efficiency policies, resource efficiency policies and the circular economy. This will include exploiting the potential of "waste to energy".

Increasing energy efficiency in the buildings sector

Heating and cooling is the largest single source of energy demand in Europe and the majority of Europe's gas imports are used for these purposes. Huge efficiency gains remain to be captured with regard to district heating and cooling, which will be addressed in a Commission strategy.

Actions by Member States, particularly at the local and regional levels, are needed to exploit the energy efficiency potential of buildings. Attracting investments at the scale needed remains a challenge, especially at the local level, mainly due to lack of awareness and expertise in small-scale financing. The Commission will support ways to simplify access to existing financing and offer 'off-the-shelf' financing templates for financial instruments to the European Structural and Investment Funds managing authorities and interested stakeholders, promote new financing schemes based on risk and revenue sharing, develop new financing techniques and support in terms of technical assistance. Financial support needs to be combined with technical support to help aggregate small-scale projects into larger programmes which can drive down transaction costs and attract the private sector at scale.

The work of the Smart Cities and Communities-initiatives as well as to the Covenant of Mayors, which are primarily carried forward by mayors, civil society organisations, investors, financial institutions and service providers, is important for achieving progress on energy efficiency in and outside the EU. This work has the Commission's firm support. The Commission will also develop a "global excellence for energy efficiency policy-making" initiative as a contribution to the G20 Energy Efficiency Action Plan. It will strongly promote the adoption of ambitious energy efficiency goals and targets in fora such as the UN "Sustainable Energy for All" initiative and the International Energy Agency. As a global leader in energy efficiency technology, this should be a driver for exports, and growth and jobs in the EU.

EU funds and EIB financing can make a huge difference. The European Fund for Strategic Investments provides an opportunity to leverage major investments in renovating buildings. Investments in this area can provide great returns in terms of growth and jobs.

Towards an energy-efficient, decarbonised transport sector

Transport represents more than 30% of final energy consumption in Europe. Realising its energy efficiency potential requires a continued focus on tightening CO_2 emission standards for passenger cars and vans post-2020, and on measures to increase fuel efficiency and reduce CO_2 emissions for heavy duty vehicles and buses. Better traffic management should also be promoted as a modern, forward-looking tool to cut CO_2 emissions.

This should be accompanied by measures to better exploit the potential of the single market and to internalise external costs. The Commission will promote the use of road charging schemes based on the polluter-pays and user-pays principles and increase efforts to create a single European transport area, based on a more optimal use of the fleet. Considerable fuel savings could also be realized by removing barriers to less green-house gas intensive modes of transport, such as rail, maritime transport and inland waterways, and by making these modes more attractive and cost efficient. The Commission will further promote the 'Shift2Rail'[23] initiative.

The Commission will also take further actions to decarbonise the transport sector, which is still essentially running on oil products. This will require a gradual transformation of the entire transport system as well as an increased development and deployment of alternative fuels. The Commission will take further action to promote the swift deployment of the necessary infrastructure, i.e. refuelling and recharging stations.[24] Market up-take of such vehicles depends on infrastructure, vehicles and fuels being rolled out together.

Electrification of transport is important to break oil dependency and to decarbonise transport, especially for road (short and medium distance) and rail transport. Europe needs to speed up electrification of its car fleet and other means of transport and become a leader in electro-mobility and energy storage technologies. This requires a full integration of electric vehicles in urban mobility policies and in the electricity grid, both as energy consumers and potential storage facilities.

2.4. Decarbonisation of the economy

An ambitious climate policy is an integral part of our Energy Union. The EU's climate policy is based on an EU-wide carbon market (the EU Emissions Trading System), ambitious but fair national green-house gas reduction targets for the sectors outside the Emissions Trading System and an energy policy to make the European Union the number one in renewable energy.

An ambitious EU Climate policy

The agreement on the 2030 climate and energy framework has defined the EU commitment of an at least 40% domestic reduction in greenhouse gas emissions compared to 1990. This makes an ambitious contribution to the international climate negotiations with a view to achieving a binding climate agreement in 2015. This contribution is spelled out in the communication on the Road to Paris, presented at the same time as this Energy Union Strategic Framework. The Commission, together with the Member States, will engage with other major economies to convince them to join Europe's ambition. It will do this through an active European climate diplomacy that makes full use of trade and development instruments.

The cornerstone of Europe's climate policy is a well-functioning EU Emissions Trading System. As a result of the Market Stability Reserve and the measures needed to meet the increased ambition decided in the 2030 framework, the EU Emissions Trading System will deliver a meaningful price on carbon emissions and stimulate cost-efficient green-house gas emission reductions. The European Commission wants the EU Emissions Trading System to fully play its role as a technology neutral, cost-effective and EU-wide driver for low-carbon investments. Through its price formation at EU level it reinforces the functioning of the internal energy market and stimulates the uptake of renewables and other low-carbon and energy-efficient technologies. Policies to prevent carbon leakage should reflect the degree of efforts undertaken in other major economies.

For the sectors not included into the EU Emissions Trading System, national targets still need to be set and the land and forestry sector will be incorporated into the EU 2030 framework, ensuring that also these sectors have the right incentives to mitigate GHG emissions and contribute to the fight against climate changes.

Becoming the number one in renewables

The European Union is committed to becoming the world leader in renewable energy, the global hub for developing the next generation of technically advanced and competitive renewable energies. The EU has also set an EU target of at least 27% for the share of renewable energy consumed in the EU in 2030.

The EU is already on track to meet its 2020 target of 20% renewable energy in its energy mix, costs for new wind and photo-voltaic capacity have reduced significantly due in large part to the EU's commitment in this area, and reform of support schemes to further drive down costs is well under way. But to achieve the 27% target, new challenges must be faced. To integrate renewable production progressively and efficiently into a market that promotes competitive renewables and drives innovation, energy markets and grids have to be fit for renewables.[25] Existing legislation and new market rules need to be fully implemented, enabling the roll-out of new technologies smart grids and demand response for an efficient energy transition.

In line with the Environmental and Energy Aid Guidelines, renewable production needs to be supported through market-based schemes that address market failures, ensure cost-effectiveness and avoid overcompensation or distortion. Low-cost financing for capital intensive renewables depends on having a stable investment framework that reduces regulatory risk. This is necessary to ensure investor confidence and to attract investments from international funds, large scale project promoters and cooperatives and households in a market-based framework that keeps capital costs down. The Commission will facilitate cooperation[26] and convergence of national support schemes leading to more cross border opening through in-depth discussions with Member States on the respective Commission Guidance[27] and the Environmental and Energy Aid Guidelines.

Investment decisions in renewable electricity have to take into account the physical realities of resource availability and of the grid; public acceptance; consumption location and administrative barriers. Also, the development of new infrastructure, especially interconnections, needs to lower the cost of integrating renewable electricity into the internal energy market.

The EU needs to invest in advanced, sustainable alternative fuels, including biofuel production processes, and in the bio-economy more generally. This allows us to retain technological and industrial leadership and to meet climate change objectives. The EU will also need to take into account the impact of bioenergy on the environment, land-use and food production. The EU Investment Plan, as well as other EU financing sources, could help to ensure the necessary financing.

2.5. An Energy Union for Research, Innovation and Competitiveness

A new strategy for Research and Innovation (R&I) must be at the very heart of the Energy Union. If Europe's Energy Union is to be the world number one in renewable energies, it must lead on the next generation of renewable technologies as well as to storage solutions.

Equally, putting the EU at the forefront of smart grid and smart home technology, clean transport, as well as clean fossil fuel and the world's safest nuclear generation, is central to the aim of turning the Energy Union into a motor for growth, jobs and competitiveness.

Although important progress has been made in improving the effectiveness of Europe's research programmes, much more can be done. We are still a long way from fully coordinated and focussed research, effectively combining EU and Member State programmes around common goals and deliverables. If we are to achieve our aims, we must get the maximum possible results from every Euro invested across the whole EU. This means taking an integrated approach to create synergies; working together to coordinate efforts and deliver results; ensuring more effective links between research and industry and thereby bringing new technologies to the market in the EU.

To achieve this, the new European energy R&I approach[28] should accelerate energy system transformation. This should build on Horizon 2020 and involve all Member States, stakeholders and the Commission.

Actions should be grouped around the following four core priorities, to which Member States and the Commission would commit:

- Being the world leader in developing the next generation of renewable energy technologies, including environment-friendly production and use of biomass and biofuels, together with energy storage;

- Facilitating the participation of consumers in the energy transition through smart grids, smart home appliances, smart cities, and home automation systems;

- Efficient energy systems, and harnessing technology to make the building stock energy neutral, and

- More sustainable transport systems that develop and deploy at large scale innovative technologies and services to increase energy efficiency and reduce greenhouse gas emissions.

On top of these four common priorities, there are additional research priorities which merit a much greater level of collaboration between the Commission and those Member States who want to use these technologies:

- A forward-looking approach to carbon capture and storage (CCS) and carbon capture and use (CCU) for the power and industrial sectors, which will be critical to reaching the 2050 climate objectives in a cost-effective way. This will require an enabling policy framework, including a reform of the Emissions Trading System and the new Innovation Fund, to increase business and investor clarity, which is needed to further develop this technology.

- Nuclear energy presently produces nearly 30% of the EU's electricity.[29] The EU must ensure that Member States use the highest standards of safety, security, waste management and non-proliferation. The EU should also ensure that it maintains technological leadership in the nuclear domain, including through ITER, so as not to increase energy and technology dependence.

An innovation-driven transition to a low carbon economy offers great opportunities for growth and jobs. New business sectors, new business models and new job profiles will emerge. Technological leadership must be followed by the development of industrial production capabilities or technology supply chains across Europe. This requires bringing together research, industry, the financing sector and public authorities. An efficient industrial strategy along these lines will enable the

EU industry to benefit from the first-mover advantage, both domestically and within international technology markets, with the resulting positive effects on competitiveness and job creation.

The Commission will explore how public procurement can exploit its potential to act as a catalyst for industrial and business innovation, and green growth both within the EU and beyond its borders. It will make full use of EU trade policy to improve access to foreign markets for Energy Union related technologies and services as well as to protect the EU market from unfair trade practices, and support other countries in their efforts to establish modern and sustainable energy systems. The Commission will work with Member States and regions to ensure synergies between the different EU funds and to exploit the full potential of Cohesion Policy funding for innovation. Change also means that some sectors, business models or job profiles will have to adjust. Vocational and other training paths for new or adapted job profiles have to be established, corresponding to the new business needs and providing people with solid professional skills. An energy transition that is just and fair will therefore require re-training or up-skilling of employees in certain sectors and, where needed, social measures at the appropriate level. The first-hand knowledge and experience of the social partners is crucial in this regard. The Commission will inform the social partners and invite them to include the energy transition in their social dialogue at European level.

3. Energy Union Governance

The Energy Union also needs an integrated governance and monitoring process, to make sure that energy-related actions at European, regional, national and local level all contribute to the Energy Union's objectives. The governance process should serve the following purposes:

- bring together energy and climate actions as well as actions in other relevant policy areas, leading to more and longer-term policy coherence. This also provides long term certainty and guidance for investors;

- secure implementation of the internal energy market and the delivery of the 2030 energy and climate framework, notably the implementation of the agreed 2030 targets on renewables, energy efficiency, non-Emissions Trading System and interconnections;

- streamline current planning and reporting requirements, avoiding unnecessary administrative burden;

- involve an energy dialogue with stakeholders to inform policy-making and support active engagement in managing the energy transition;

- deepen the cooperation between Member States, including at the regional level, and with the Commission;

- improve the data, analysis and intelligence needed to underpin the Energy Union by pooling the relevant knowledge and making it easily accessible to all stakeholders, and

- annual reporting to the European Parliament and the Council on the state of the Energy Union in order to address the key issues and steer the policy debate.

The Commission will launch a dynamic governance process for the European Energy Union. While there will be clear links between this governance process and the European Semester, the two processes will be managed separately.

4. Delivering the Energy Union

Achieving the Energy Union means delivering on the actions set out in this Strategy, which are summarised in the fifteen points set out below. The attached roadmap shows the initiatives to be developed as part of the Strategy, with a clear timetable for adoption and implementation as well as respective responsibilities. The Commission regards these as inter-linked and consistent with the scale of ambition the EU needs to transform Europe's energy system.

Successful implementation depends on the political commitment of all actors concerned, including EU institutions, Member States, the European Investment Bank and other stakeholders, including at regional and local level, in line with the principles of subsidiarity, proportionality and better regulation.

The EU must be able to react to unexpected events, seize new opportunities and anticipate and adapt to future trends. Whenever necessary, the Commission will use its right of initiative to set out an appropriate response to events.

The Commission invites the European Parliament and Council to endorse this strategy to deliver the Energy Union and to actively engage in its implementation, in close cooperation with all relevant stakeholders.

The Energy Union in fifteen action points

1. Full implementation and strict enforcement of existing energy and related legislation is the first priority to establish the Energy Union.
   > The Commission will use all instruments to ensure that Member States fully implement energy legislation, in particular the 3rd Internal Energy Market Package, and it will strictly enforce the Treaty's competition rules.

2. The EU needs to diversify its supply of gas and make it more resilient to supply disruptions.
   > The Commission will propose a resilience and diversification package for gas in 2015-2016 by revising the existing security of gas supply Regulation.
   > The Commission will prepare a comprehensive strategy for liquid natural gas (LNG) and its storage, and
   > The Commission will work with Member States to develop access to alternative suppliers, including from the Southern Gas Corridor route, the Mediterranean and Algeria, in order to decrease existing dependencies on individual suppliers.

3. Intergovernmental agreements should comply fully with EU legislation and be more transparent.
   > The Commission will propose a revision of the Decision on Intergovernmental Agreements in 2016 to ensure compatibility with EU legislation before agreements are negotiated, involve the Commission in such negotiations, develop standard contract clauses covering EU rules and make commercial gas supply contracts more transparent.

4. The right infrastructure is a precondition for completing the energy market, integrating renewables and security of supply.
   > The Commission will support the implementation of major infrastructure projects, particularly the Projects of Common Interest, through the available financial means, e.g. the Connecting Europe Facility, the European Structural

and Investment Funds and the future European Fund for Strategic Investments to leverage the necessary private and public funding.

> The Commission will bring together information on EU-funded infrastructure projects to bring more coherence and to maximise their impact.

> The Commission will create a dedicated Energy Infrastructure Forum to discuss progress on major infrastructure projects with Member States, regional cooperation groups and EU institutions. It will meet for the first time in late 2015.

5. Creating a seamless internal energy market that benefits citizens, ensuring security of supply, integrating renewables in the market and remedying the currently uncoordinated development of capacity mechanisms in Member States call for a review of the current market design.
   > The Commission will propose legislation on security of supply for electricity in 2016.
   > The Commission will propose a new European electricity market design in 2015, which will be followed by legislative proposals in 2016.

6. The regulatory framework set-up by the 3rd Internal Energy Market Package has to be further developed to deliver a seamless internal energy market to citizens and companies.
   > The Commission will review the regulatory framework, in particular the functioning of ACER and the ENTSOs, in 2015-2016 and will propose appropriate actions to reinforce the European regulatory framework.

7. Regional approaches to market integration are an important part of the move towards a fully integrated EU-wide energy market.
   > The Commission will develop guidance on regional cooperation and engage actively in regional cooperation bodies with Member States and stakeholders.

8. Greater transparency on energy costs and prices as well as on the level of public support will enhance market integration and identify actions that distort the internal market.

> The Commission will produce biennial reports on energy prices, analyse in depth the role of taxes, levies and subsidies and seek the phasing out of regulated prices below cost.
> At the national and local levels, action should be taken to protect vulnerable consumers through social policies.

9. The EU has set itself the target of reaching at least 27% energy savings by 2030.
> In 2015 and 2016, the Commission will review all relevant energy efficiency legislation and will propose revisions, where needed, to underpin the 2030 target.
> Member States and regions should make more use of European funds for renovation of housing.

10. Buildings have huge potential for energy efficiency gains. Retrofitting existing buildings to make them energy efficient and making full use of sustainable space heating and cooling will reduce the EU's energy import bills, reinforce energy security and cut energy costs for households and businesses.
> The Commission will develop a 'Smart Financing for Smart Buildings'-initiative to make existing buildings more energy-efficient, facilitating access to existing funding instruments.
> The Commission will propose a strategy to facilitate investment in heating and cooling.

11. The EU needs to speed up energy efficiency and decarbonisation in the transport sector, its progressive switch to alternative fuels and the integration of the energy and transport systems.
> The Commission will propose a comprehensive road transport package promoting more efficient pricing of infrastructure, the roll-out of intelligent transport solutions and enhancing energy efficiency.
> The Commission will take further action to create the right market conditions for an increased deployment of alternative fuels and to further promote procurement of clean vehicles. This will be delivered through a mix of national, regional and local measures, supported by the EU.

12. The EU agreed a climate and energy framework for 2030 at the October European Council. This now needs to be implemented. The EU will provide an ambitious contribution to the international climate negotiations.
    > The Commission will propose legislation to achieve the greenhouse gas reduction target agreed at the October 2014 European Council both in the Emissions Trading System and in the sectors outside the Emissions Trading System.

13. The EU has agreed the target of at least 27% at EU level for renewable energy by 2030.
    > The Commission will propose a new Renewable Energy Package in 2016-2017. This will include a new policy for sustainable biomass and biofuels as well as legislation to ensure that the 2030 EU target is met cost-effectively.

14. The EU needs to develop a forward-looking, energy and climate-related R&I strategy to maintain European technological leadership and expand export opportunities.
    > The Commission will propose a European energy R&I approach, comprising an upgraded Strategic Energy Technology Plan and a strategic transport R&I agenda, with a limited number of essential priorities and clear objectives, in 2015-2016.
    > The Commission will develop an initiative on global technology and innovation leadership on energy and climate to boost jobs and growth.

15. The EU will use all external policy instruments to ensure that a strong, united EU engages constructively with its partners and speaks with one voice on energy and climate.
    > The Commission, with the HR/VP, and the Member States will revitalise the EU's energy and climate diplomacy.
    > The Commission, with the HR/VP, will develop an active agenda to strengthen EU energy cooperation with third countries, including on renewable energy and energy efficiency.

The Commission will make full use of the EU's external trade policy to promote access to energy resources and to foreign markets for European energy technology and services.

Notes

1 Communication "Energy Efficiency and its contribution to energy security and the 2030 Framework for climate and energy policy", COM(2014)520.

2 European Energy Security Strategy, COM (2014) 330.

3 Commission estimates. The IEA estimates that EUR 1.3 trillion are needed by 2025 in generation, transport and distribution.

4 Calculations of DG Energy based on Platts market reports and IEA data for first half of 2014.

5 Eur'Observeur 2014 report.

6 Compared to a 32% EU share in overall global patents.

7 UNEP-BNEF Global Trends in Renewable Energy Investments 2014.

8 COM (2014)330.

9 EU leadership will continue to drive standards and efficiency improvements globally, reducing future oil consumption and thus EU dependency.

10 Directive 2009/119/EC of 14 September 2009 imposing an obligation on Member States to maintain minimum stocks of crude oil and/or petroleum products.

11 COM(2014) 654 final.

12 See the Communication "Making the most of public interventions", C(2013)7243.

13 Initiatives such as "trade in green goods" will help promote products that help reduce CO2 emissions, benefit the environment and create EU jobs and growth.

14 Decision No 994/2012/EU establishing an information exchange mechanism with regard to intergovernmental agreements between Member States and third countries in the field of energy.

15 This update will include strategic Projects of Energy Community Interest (PECIs) that are important to enhance the Energy Union's security of supply, if they also comply with the criteria to become PCIs.

16 EU Investment Plan, COM(2014)903.

17 Examples for this could be decisions relating to new infrastructure affecting more than two Member States, on exemptions from physical reverse flows in line with the Security of Gas Supply Regulation, cross-border cost allocations under the TEN-E Regulation or similar.

18 See the Communication "Making the most of public interventions", C(2013)7243.

19 Environmental and Energy State Aid Guidelines (EEAG), OJ C 200, 28.6.2014, p. 1-55.

20 The application of EEAG to the support schemes approved to date has partly mitigated the effects of fragmentation, however, further action is needed.

21 See the resource efficiency roadmap (COM(2011)571) and the 2012 Communication on the internal energy market (COM(2012)663), and in line with the G20 commitment.

22 See Report "Benchmarking smart metering deployment in the EU-27 with a focus on electricity", COM(2014)356.

23 Regulation 642/2014 establishing the Shift2Rail Joint Undertaking.

24 Directive 2014/94/EU of the European Parliament and of the Council of 22 October 2014 on the deployment of alternative fuels infrastructure.

25 Making markets fit for renewables means short term markets need to develop into deep, liquid and real time functioning. Existing power grids designed and often managed for conventional power production in a national scope are suboptimal for a future where supply from renewable sources will become ever more important and where balancing is needed to compensate for their inherent variability.

26 Several Member States are looking into using cooperation mechanisms from the Renewable Energy Directive to meet their national targets cost-efficiently. The Commission has been supporting this process by helping Member States to find solutions for technical and financial issues related to these cross-border mechanisms.

27 European Commission guidance for the design of renewables support schemes, SWD(2013)439; Guidance on the use of renewable energy cooperation mechanism, SWD(2013)440.

28 This should comprise an updated Strategic Energy Technology Plan and a strategic transport R&I agenda.

29 See European Energy Security Strategy, COM (2014) 330.

Annex to Appendix 1

Energy Union Package

Annex

Roadmap for the Energy Union

A Framework Strategy for a Resilient Energy Union with a Forward-Looking Climate Change Policy

Communication from the Commission to the European Parliament, the Council, the European Economic and Social Committee of the regions and the European Investment bank

COM(2015) 80 final, Annex 1, 25.2.2015

Actions	Respon-sible party	Time-table	SoS	IEM	EE	GHG	R&I
Infrastructure							
Effective implemen-tation of the 10% electricity intercon-nection target	Commission Member States National Regulatory Authorities Transmis-sion System Operators	2015-20	X	X		X	
2nd list of Projects of Common Interest (PCI) - leading to Commission Del-egated Act	Commission Member States	2015	X	X		X	
Communication on the progress to-wards the comple-tion of the list of the most vital energy infrastructures and on the necessary measures to reach the 15% electric-ity interconnection target for 2030	Commission	2016	X	X			
Establish an Energy Infrastructure Forum	Commission Member States	2015	X	X			

Actions	Respon-sible party	Time-table	SoS	IEM	EE	GHG	R&I
Electricity							
Initiative on market design and regional electricity markets, and coordination of capacities to ensure security of supply, boosting cross-border trade and facilitating integration of renewable energy	Commission	2015-2016	X	X	X	X	
Review of the Directive concerning measures to safeguard security of electricity supply	Commission	2016	X	X		X	

Actions	Respon-sible party	Time-table	SoS	IEM	EE	GHG	R&I
Retail							
New Deal for energy consumers: Empowering con-sumers, deploying Demand Side Re-sponse; using smart technology; linking wholesale and retail markets; phase-out of regulated prices; flanking measures to protect vulner-able customers	Commission Member States	2015-2016		X	X	X	X
Gas							
Revision of the Regulation on secu-rity of gas supply	Commission	2015-2016	X	X			
Liquified Natural Gas and storage strategy	Commission	2015-2016	X				
Regulatory framework							
Review of the Agency for the Cooperation of Energy Regulators (ACER) and the energy regulatory framework	Commission	2015-16	X	X		X	

Appendix Energy Union Package COM(2015) 80 final, 25.2.2015

Actions	Respon-sible party	Time-table	SoS	IEM	EE	GHG	R&I
Renewables							
Renewable Energy Package: including a new Renewable Energy Directive for 2030; best practices in renewable energy self-consumption and support schemes; bioenergy sustainability policy.	Commission	2015-2017	X	X		X	
Communication on Waste to Energy	Commission	2016	X			X	
Climate Action							
Legislative proposal to revise the EU Emissions Trading System, 2021-2030	Commission	2015	X	X		X	
Legislative proposals on the Effort-Sharing Decision and the inclusion of Land Use, Land Use Change and Forestry (LULUCF) into the 2030 Climate and Energy Framework	Commission	2016				X	

Actions	**Respon-sible party**	**Time-table**	**SoS**	**IEM**	**EE**	**GHG**	**R&I**
Transport actions							
Fair and efficient pricing for sustain-able transport – revision of the Eu-rovignette Directive and framework to promote European electronic tolling	Commission	2016			X	X	
Review of market access rules for road transport to improve its energy efficiency	Commission	2016			X	X	
Master Plan for the deployment of Co-operative Intelligent Transport Systems	Commission Member States Industry	2016			X	X	X
Review of Regu-lations setting emission perfor-mance standards to establish post-2020 targets for cars and vans	Commission	2016 - 2017			X	X	X

Actions	Respon-sible party	Time-table	SoS	IEM	EE	GHG	R&I
Establishing a monitoring and reporting system for heavy duty vehicles (trucks and buses) with a view to improving purchaser information	Commission	2016-2017			X	X	X
Review of Directive on the Promotion of Clean and Energy Efficient Road Transport Vehicles	Commission	2017			X	X	
Communication on decarbonising the transport sector, including an action plan on second and third generation biofuels and other alternative, sustainable fuels	Commission	2017			X	X	X
Energy efficiency							
Review of the Energy Efficiency Directive	Commission	2016	X		X	X	X

Actions	Respon-sible party	Time-table	SoS	IEM	EE	GHG	R&I
Review of the Directive on Energy Performance of Buildings includ-ing Smart Finance for Smart Buildings initiative	Commission	2016	X		X	X	X
Review of the energy efficiency framework for products (Energy Labelling Directive and Ecodesign Directives)	Commission	2015	X		X	X	X
Strengthening the targeted use of fi-nancial instruments to support invest-ments in energy efficiency	Commission	2015-			X	X	
Heating and Cooling							
EU strategy for Heating and Cool-ing - the contribu-tion from heating and cooling in realising the EU's energy and climate objectives	Commission	2015	X	X	X	X	X

Appendix Energy Union Package COM(2015) 80 final, 25.2.2015

Actions	Respon-sible party	Time-table	SoS	IEM	EE	GHG	R&I
External Energy and Climate Policy							
EU Energy and Climate policy diplomacy	Commission HR/VP Member States	2015	X	X		X	X
Review of the Deci-sion on information exchange mecha-nism with regard to intergovernmen-tal agreements between Member States and third countries in the field of energy	Commission HR/VP	2016	X	X			
New and strength-ened energy dialogues with countries of impor-tance for EU energy policy	Commission HR/VP	2015 -	X	X	X	X	X
Memorandum of Understanding on an upgraded strate-gic partnership with Ukraine	Commission HR/VP European Parliament Council	2015	X	X			

Actions	Respon-sible party	Time-table	SoS	IEM	EE	GHG	R&I
Trilateral Memorandum of Understanding on the Trans-Caspian pipelines with Azerbaijan and Turkmenistan	Commission HR/VP European Parliament Council	2015	X	X			
Initiative to strengthen the Energy Community	Commission Energy Community Contracting Parties HR/VP	2015	X	X			
Strengthen Euromed cooperation on gas, electricity, energy efficiency and renewables	Commission HR/VP	2015-2016	X	X			
Adoption and signature of a new International Energy Charter on behalf of the EU and EURATOM	Commission HR/VP	2015	X	X			

Actions	Respon-sible party	Time-table	SoS	IEM	EE	GHG	R&I
Industrial competitiveness							
A new European energy R&I approach to accelerate energy system transformation, composed of - an integrated Strategic Energy Technology (SET) Plan - a strategic transport R&I agenda	Commission	2015-2017					X
Analysis of energy prices and costs (including taxes and subsidies)	Commission	2016 and every 2 years thereafter		X			
Initiative on EU global technology and innovation leadership on energy and climate to boost growth and jobs	Commission	2015-2016			X	X	X
Enhanced trade policy to facilitate export of EU technologies	Commission	2015-2019	X	X			X

Actions	Responsible party	Timetable	SoS	IEM	EE	GHG	R&I
Cross cutting measures							
Review of the Guidelines on State aid for environmental protection and energy	Commission	2017-2019	X	X	X	X	X
Report on the European Energy Security Strategy; including a platform and roadmap for Euromed and strategies for LNG, energy storage, and the Southern gas corridor	Commission	2015-2016	X	X	X	X	X
Data, analysis and intelligence for the Energy Union: initiative pooling and making easily accessible all relevant knowledge in the Commission and Member States	Commission	2016	X	X	X	X	X

Actions	Respon-sible party	Time-table	SoS	IEM	EE	GHG	R&I
Nuclear							
Council Regulation updating the information requirements of Article 41 of the Euratom Treaty in the light of the European Energy Security Strategy	Commission	2015	X	X			
Communication on a nuclear illustrative programme (PINC) pursuing Article 40 of the Euratom Treaty	Commission	2015	X			X	